Pathways

What you believe really matters!

For individuals or groups

By Dr. Stan Fleming
Gate Breaker Ministries
Meridian, Idaho

Introduction to the Pathways Devotional

Welcome to the Pathways course! It is my hope that it will be a blessing to you and a time to strengthen your walk with the Lord Jesus Christ.

Our walk with the Lord can be compared to a pathway on which He leads us. So, this course is based upon the theme of Pathways. They lead us somewhere. The choice of which pathway we take in life is often influenced by the things that we believe and the teachings that we embrace. Each lesson will begin with a Scripture emphasizing this theme.

As Christians, we have the privilege (1) to experience all that Christ has for us, (2) to grow in relationship with Him and other Christians, and (3) to understand the basic but important beliefs and doctrines emphasized in the Bible. The knowledge of these things helps us to find the best path for our lives. May God bless you richly in this course!

This course is designed for either individual or group study method. Individuals may use it for devotional purposes. It may also be used for small or large groups. It is facilitator friendly! See the supplementary information page for more details.

- Dr. Stan Fleming

Ponder the path of your feet, and let all your ways be established. – Proverbs 4:26

Jesus said to him, "I am the way, the truth, and the life. No one comes to the Father except through Me." – John 14:6

Supplementary Information

Overview: This is a course about basic Christian beliefs and practical living. It considers (1) the greatest commandments about love, (2) historic Christian beliefs, which are primarily about God, (3) the importance of abiding in the doctrine of Christ, (4) the principles of Christ, which essentially are teachings about man's salvation, service to God, and the outcome of how we live, and (5) the practical side of everyday Christian living.

Note to individuals: This eight-part course can easily be used for individual devotional or study purposes. Lessons can be divided into weekly or periodical devotionals. Activity and discussion questions are sometimes introspective, so individuals can simply meditate on these. Other questions refer back to answers found in the Scripture passages just read.

Note to group leaders / facilitators: Each lesson contains numerous passages, ideas, and questions. Depending on the time allotted for the lesson, the leader may use all of the material or select certain sections but ask the members to read the other sections at home on their own time. Another approach would be to visit all of the sections but to limit

3

the time spent on each one. It is a good idea to give a brief overview before launching into each lesson. There are activities at the beginning of each lesson which may help facilitate discussion and introduce the concepts. The facilitator may choose as many as practical to participate in the activity.

Opening Prayer: The beginning of each lesson includes a biblical passage that associates the concept of a way or pathway in our lives. Use this for introductory prayer. For instance, individuals doing a weekly devotional can use the first lesson's passage "Follow the way of love" - 1st Corinthians 14:1 (NIV) to begin each devotional time on that subject. Facilitators can use it if they desire to open up the session in prayer. Use what works best for you.

Table of Contents

Pathways was created and written by Dr. Stan Fleming.
Gate Breaker Ministries
Meridian, Idaho, USA
Gatebreakers.com
2017

1: The Greatest Commandments

Follow the way of love. – 1 Corinthians 14:1 (NIV)

Activity: Consider a time when the love of God or someone's love impacted you in a positive way. Have several people share about it.

WHAT ARE THE GREATEST COMMANDMENTS?

The Lord Jesus taught us that the greatest commandments are all about love.

1. *But when the Pharisees heard that He had silenced the Sadducees, they gathered together. 35 Then one of them, a lawyer, asked Him a question, testing Him, and saying, 36 "Teacher, which is the great commandment in the law?" 37 Jesus said to him, "'You shall love the LORD your God with all your heart, with all your soul, and with all your mind.' 38 This is the first and great commandment. 39 And the second is like it: 'You shall love your neighbor as yourself.' 40 On these two commandments hang all the Law and the Prophets."* - Matthew 22:34-40

2. *Then one of the scribes came, and having heard them reasoning together, perceiving that He had answered them well, asked Him, "Which is the first commandment of all?" 29 Jesus answered him, "The first of all the commandments is: 'Hear, O Israel, the LORD our God, the LORD is one. 30 And you shall love the LORD your God with all your heart, with all your soul, with all your mind, and with all your strength.' This is the first commandment. 31 And the second, like it, is this: 'You shall love your neighbor as yourself.' There is no other commandment greater than these."* - Mark 12:28-31

3. *Hear, O Israel: The LORD our God, the LORD is one! 5 You shall love the LORD your God with all your heart, with all*

7

your soul, and with all your strength. 6 "And these words which I command you today shall be in your heart. 7 You shall teach them diligently to your children, and shall talk of them when you sit in your house, when you walk by the way, when you lie down, and when you rise up. 8 You shall bind them as a sign on your hand, and they shall be as frontlets between your eyes. 9 You shall write them on the doorposts of your house and on your gates. – Deuteronomy 6:4-9

Questions / Considerations:

- What is the greatest commandment? What is the second greatest commandment?

- In the passage from Matthew, why did the lawyer ask Jesus the question? What do you think his motive was?

- The passages in Matthew, Mark, and Deuteronomy emphasize slightly different aspects of human responsibility in loving God. What are the differences?

- Consider the emphasis placed upon the Israelites in the Deuteronomy passage of the daily importance of loving God. How does this apply to our lives today as Christians? How can we remind ourselves more often to show our love and affection for God?

- The Lord seems to have no reservations about stressing the rule (commandment) that we should communicate love to God and others.

- The Law and the Prophets: Romans 13:8-10 lists six of the Ten Commandments found in Exodus 20:1-17. These six commandments correspond with those that refer to how we treat other people. Of the Ten Commandments, the first four refer to how we should treat (love) God and the last six refer to how we should treat (love) our neighbor.

GOD LOVES US

There are many passages about God's love for people. The fact that He created people in His image and likeness and then blessed them presupposes His love for people (Genesis 1:26-28). Notice the word "lovingkindness" in the Old Testament verses below. The Hebrew word *checed* is described as steadfast love, grace, mercy, faithfulness, goodness, and devotion. It is one of God's most fundamental characteristics.

1. *How precious is Your <u>lovingkindness</u>, O God! Therefore, the children of men put their trust under the shadow of Your wings.* – Psalm 36:7

2. *Because Your <u>lovingkindness</u> is better than life, My lips shall praise You.* – Psalm 63:3

3. *Hear me, O LORD, for Your <u>lovingkindness</u> is good; Turn to me according to the multitude of Your tender mercies.* – Psalm 69:16

4. *For God so loved the world that He gave His only begotten Son, that whoever believes in Him should not perish but have everlasting life. 17 For God did not send His Son into the world to condemn the world, but that the world through Him might be saved.* – John 3:16-17

5. *We love Him because He first loved us.* – 1 John 4:19

Questions / Considerations:

- When people really come to understand that God loves them, it can transform their lives, give them a whole new purpose for living, and impact not only their destiny but that of generations to come. Have you had a revelation of God's love for you?

BIBLICAL CONCEPTS ABOUT LOVE

The basic biblical concept about love is three-fold:

1. God loves us.

2. We are to love God.

3. We are to love one another.

The word *love* has different ideas and definitions. In the New Testament it can be a verb (action word): "God loves you". It can be a noun (a person or thing): "God is love" (1 John 4:8, 16). As a thing, the word *love* in the Greek can be considered godly (*agape*), brotherly (*phileo*), or express the physical intimacy between spouses (*eros*). Love is a fruit of the spirit (Galatians 5:22) and love is the greatest gift (1 Corinthians 1:13). In modern society the word *love* is referred to as an emotion, or it may be more accurate to say that it relates to a range of human emotions that convey various feelings, states, or attitudes. People might say that they love some type of food or activity, but they do not mean it in the same sense as loving a person or God. The Bible teaches that Christians should have godly love for all people.

THE CHARACTERISTICS OF LOVE

The ideas about love stated in the Bible often express an underlying nature of strength and even miraculous power:

1. **Strength of love:** *For love is as strong as death.*- Song of Solomon 8:6

2. **Perfect love:** *Perfect love casts out fear.* – 1 John 4:18

3. **Fervent love:** *And above all things have fervent love for one another, for love will cover a multitude of sins.* – 1 Peter 4:8

4. **Definition:** *Love suffers long and is kind; love does not envy; love does not parade itself, is not puffed up; 5 does not behave rudely, does not seek its own, is not provoked, thinks no evil; 6 does not rejoice in iniquity, but rejoices in the truth; 7 bears all things, believes all things, hopes all things, endures all things. 8 Love never fails.* – 1 Corinthians 13:4-8

5. **Works for our good:** (TLB) *And we know that all that happens to us is working for our good if we love God and are fitting into his plans.* – Romans 8:28

Questions / Considerations:

- Can you remember a time in which the strength of love carried you through a difficult situation?

- How do you think that love counteracts fear, covers sin, or is able to suffer long? Is it because of the miraculous nature of love?

- How does love work out in the real world? For instance, are there practical ways that we can apply the idea that love "believes all things" and "hopes all things" when confronted by people which experience has taught us might try to deceive, take advantage, or even do harm? Since Jesus as the embodiment of love sometimes confronted people head on about things (i.e. confronting Pharisees and money changers), can we learn from His actions how love might interact in a fallen world? Perhaps part of the answer lies in remembering that the greatest commandment is to love God.

GOD'S LOVE AND THE CIRCUMSTANCES OF LIFE

We can learn some insight into the perspective of early Christians from two of the Apostle Paul's passages about love. In the first passage he asks a rhetorical question and in the second he offers a prayer.

1. *Who shall separate us from the love of Christ? Shall tribulation, or distress, or persecution, or famine, or nakedness, or peril, or sword? 36 As it is written: "For Your sake we are killed all day long; We are accounted as sheep for the slaughter." 37 Yet in all these things we are more than conquerors through Him who loved us. 38 For I am persuaded that neither death nor life, nor angels nor principalities nor*

powers, nor things present nor things to come, 39 nor height nor depth, nor any other created thing, shall be able to separate us from the love of God which is in Christ Jesus our Lord. – Romans 8:35-39

2. *For this reason I bow my knees to the Father of our Lord Jesus Christ, 15 from whom the whole family in heaven and earth is named, 16 that He would grant you, according to the riches of His glory, to be strengthened with might through His Spirit in the inner man, 17 that Christ may dwell in your hearts through faith; that you, being rooted and grounded in love, 18 may be able to comprehend with all the saints what is the width and length and depth and height -- 19 to know the love of Christ which passes knowledge; that you may be filled with all the fullness of God.* – Ephesians 3:14-19

Questions / Considerations:

- Paul is persuaded of what? So, the early Christians believed that nothing could separate them from the love of Christ.

- In the Ephesians' passage, the idea is presented that when we get rooted and grounded in God's love, we can begin to comprehend the enormity of it. Yet, in the end it is larger than our knowledge (our ability to fully know).

- In the early Church, Christians began from the premise that God loved them first and foremost regardless of what circumstances they were going through (i.e. tribulation, persecution, and sword). This helped them respond to the circumstances from a God – centered perspective. Today, people often begin from the wrong perspective. They look at difficult life situations and then question whether God loves or cares for them based upon that hardship. Christians, too, sometime begin from the wrong perspective. We, along with all of the saints, should recognize that nothing can separate us from His love. We are always in the midst of it. It is greater than what our limited reasoning can really grasp.

LOVING OUR NEIGHBOR

One of the New Testament reports about the greatest commandments comes when a lawyer wants to justify himself. Jesus responds with the Parable of the Good Samaritan.

1. (TLB) *One day an expert on Moses' laws came to test Jesus' orthodoxy by asking him this question: "Teacher, what does a man need to do to live forever in heaven?" 26 Jesus replied, "What does Moses' law say about it?" 27 "It says," he replied, "that you must love the Lord your God with all your heart, and with all your soul, and with all your strength, and with all your mind. And you must love your neighbor just as much as you love yourself." 28 "Right!" Jesus told him. "Do this and you shall live!" 29 The man wanted to justify (his lack of love for some kinds of people), so he asked, "Which neighbors?" 30 Jesus replied with an illustration: "A Jew going on a trip from Jerusalem to Jericho was attacked by bandits. They stripped him of his clothes and money, and beat him up and left him lying half dead beside the road. 31 "By chance a Jewish priest came along; and when he saw the man lying there, he crossed to the other side of the road and passed him by. 32 A Jewish Temple-assistant walked over and looked at him lying there, but then went on. 33 "But a despised Samaritan came along, and when he saw him, he felt deep pity. 34 Kneeling beside him the Samaritan soothed his wounds with medicine and bandaged them. Then he put the man on his donkey and walked along beside him till they came to an inn, where he nursed him through the night. 35 The next day he handed the innkeeper two twenty-dollar bills and told him to take care of the man. 'If his bill runs higher than that,' he said, 'I'll pay the difference the next time I am here.' 36 "Now which of these three would you say was a neighbor to the bandits' victim?" 37 The man replied, "The one who showed him some pity." Then Jesus said, "Yes, now go and do the same. – Luke 10:25-37*

Questions / Considerations:

- Why did the lawyer try to justify himself and ask the question about which neighbors? Did the lawyer consider the Samaritan an enemy? How does that apply to society today?

- Jesus often used illustrations and questions to pierce the deeper issues of the heart. Why do you think that this method was so effective in this situation? What did the illustration expose about the lawyer's probable idea of a neighbor?

- There are allusions in the illustration of the problems between the Jews and Samaritans, as well as other theological implications. For instance, notice the difference in the three people that came upon the victim. However, for our purpose, what does the story basically show about how we, as the Lord's servants, should live among and treat our neighbors?

LOVE IN THE HOME

Love in the family is one of the most important parts of Christian life. God's creation of marriage, children, and the ideas of nurturing, honor, love, and respect that should be in family life are throughout the Bible. Consider the following passages.

1. *Then He said, "Take now your son, <u>your only son Isaac, whom you love.</u>* – Genesis 22:2

2. *So Jacob served seven years for Rachel, and they seemed only a few days to him because of the <u>love he had for her</u>.* – Genesis 29:20

3. *And rejoice with the wife of your youth . . . And always <u>be enraptured with her love</u>.* - Proverbs 5:18-19

4. *How fair is your love, my sister, my spouse! How much better than wine is your love.* - Song 4:10

5. *So husbands ought to <u>love</u> their own wives as their own bodies; he who loves his wife loves himself.* - Ephesians 5:28

6. *Nevertheless, let each one of you in particular so <u>love</u> his own wife as himself, and let the wife see that she <u>respects</u> her husband.* – Ephesians 5:33

7. (TLB) *Children, obey your parents; this is the right thing to do because God has placed them in authority over you. 2 <u>Honor your father and mother</u>. This is the first of God's Ten Commandments that ends with a promise. 3 And this is the promise: that if you honor your father and mother, yours will be a long life, full of blessing. 4 And now a word to you parents. Don't keep on scolding and nagging your children, making them angry and resentful. <u>Rather, bring them up with the loving discipline the Lord himself approves</u>, with suggestions and godly advice.* – Ephesians 6:1-4

8. *Admonish the <u>young women to love their husbands, to love their children</u>.* – Titus 2:4

Questions / Considerations:

- Consider the issues of love, respect, honor, loving discipline and the needs in the modern Christian home. Why are these things so important? Whenever you feel inadequate in these areas, remember that every person falls short at times in loving others, even in our families. However, God loves us and loves our families. We need to ask Him to help us to express His love in the best way possible. He will!

- Today, families are sometimes blended with children from different parents, or single parents raising children, or even grandparents raising grandchildren. Having a strong sense of God's love in the middle of the family unit has never been more important! God's love can bring strength, healing, and hope to any family or individual.

2: Historic Christian Beliefs

Therefore, brethren, having boldness to enter the Holiest by the blood of Jesus, by a new and living way which He consecrated for us, through the veil, that is, His flesh. – Hebrews 10:19-20

Activity: What is one area of positive change that has happened in your life since you accepted Christ and began to follow His ways?

THE IMPORTANCE OF WHAT PEOPLE BELIEVE

Belief is a powerful motivator for how people live their lives. What we believe shapes our thoughts and affects our activities and goals in life. If we believe something is true, we adhere to it; if we believe something is false, we reject it. Every person believes things about themselves, others, the world around them, and God. It is in what we believe and how we are mobilized by that belief that the choices are made which determine the path on which we travel. Consider the importance of belief in the following passages:

1. (NIV) *Abram believed the LORD, and he credited it to him as righteousness.* – Genesis 15:6

2. *Then the LORD said to Moses, "Reach out your hand and take it by the tail" (and he reached out his hand and caught it, and it became a rod in his hand), 5 "that they may believe that the LORD God of their fathers, the God of Abraham, the God of Isaac, and the God of Jacob, has appeared to you.* – Exodus 4:4-5

3. *I would have lost heart, unless I had believed that I would see the goodness of the LORD in the land of the living.* – Psalm 27:13

4. *Blessed is she who believed, for there will be a fulfillment of those things which were told her from the Lord.* – Luke 1:45

16

5. *Jesus said to him, "Go your way; your son lives." <u>So, the man believed</u> the word that Jesus spoke to him, and he went his way. 51 And as he was now going down, his servants met him and told him, saying, "Your son lives!"* – John 4:50-51

6. *If you confess with your mouth the Lord Jesus and believe in your heart that God has raised Him from the dead, you will be saved. 10 For <u>with the heart one believes unto righteousness</u>, and with the mouth confession is made unto salvation.* – Romans 10:9-10

7. *But without faith it is impossible to please Him, for <u>he who comes to God must believe that He is, and that He is a rewarder of those who diligently seek Him</u>.* – Hebrews 11:6

Questions / Considerations:

- Why was belief so necessary in these cases? What were the benefits or fruits of belief in each of these?

- The opposite of belief would be unbelief. What do you think the outcome of some of these situations would have been without belief?

- Have you ever gone on a trust walk? It can be called by different names but the idea is to blindfold one person while another sighted person guides them by the hand and the voice, telling the trusting person where to step, where to turn, how to proceed, etc. The blindfolded individual must put their trust, confidence, and belief in the sighted person's ability to guide them safely. This is how we are with God. There are things that we must just put our belief in because He told us to do so.

IMPORTANT DOCTRINES TO BELIEVE

The importance of sound doctrine cannot be overemphasized. The word *doctrine* means teaching or group of teachings. Learning about doctrine may not be one's favorite thing to do, but an education of teachings based on truth about God, Christianity, and the Bible can create right thinking and in turn a correct biblical world view; this helps orient one's life. It is like a lost soul finding a compass, a good roadmap, and a brief study on how to use them correctly. With these, he can find the right way. While various denominations, independent churches, and movements of Christianity may have differing views over certain doctrines such as heaven, hell, eschatology, baptisms, and other, it is in what they agree upon that shows a greater unity for the body of Christ in the world.

In this lesson we will consider eight historic Christian beliefs that many consider are essential to the Christian faith. These beliefs can also be called doctrines because they are based on teachings in Scripture. Below is the brief list which Christians have embraced and believed since the early years of the Church. The first five are about the life, person, and ministry of Jesus Christ; the sixth is about the nature of God; the seventh is about salvation; and the eighth item is about the Bible. In the sections following this, Scriptures and remarks will be given to support these beliefs.

THESE DOCTRINES ARE PRIMARILY ABOUT GOD AND HIS RESPONSE TO MANKIND'S FALLEN CONDITION.

1. The virgin birth of Jesus Christ.
2. The substitutionary atonement of Jesus Christ's death.
3. The literal resurrection of Jesus Christ from the dead.
4. The literal return of Jesus Christ.
5. The deity of Jesus Christ.
6. The Trinity
7. Salvation is a gift that comes through faith in Jesus Christ alone.
8. The inspiration of the Bible.

THE VIRGIN BIRTH OF JESUS CHRIST

The miracle of the Jesus' birth was that He was born to the Virgin Mary.

1. (NIV) *The virgin will be with child and will give birth to a son, and will call him Immanuel.* – Isaiah 7:14

2. *Now the birth of Jesus Christ was as follows: After His mother Mary was betrothed to Joseph, <u>before they came together, she was found with child of the Holy Spirit</u>. . . . 22 So all this was done that it might be fulfilled which was spoken by the Lord through the prophet, saying: 23 "Behold, the virgin shall be with child, and bear a Son, and they shall call His name Immanuel," which is translated, "God with us." 24 Then Joseph, being aroused from sleep, did as the angel of the Lord commanded him and took to him his wife, 25 <u>and did not know her till she had brought forth her firstborn Son</u>. And he called His name JESUS.* – Matthew 1:18, 22-25

3. *Now in the sixth month the angel Gabriel was sent by God to a city of Galilee named Nazareth, 27 to a virgin betrothed to a man whose name was Joseph, of the house of David. The virgin's name was Mary. 28 And having come in, the angel said to her, "Rejoice, highly favored one, the Lord is with you; blessed are you among women!" . . . The Holy Spirit will come upon you, and the power of the Highest will overshadow you; therefore, also, that Holy One who is to be born will be called the Son of God.* – Luke 1:26-28, 35

THE SUBSTITUTIONARY ATONEMENT OF JESUS CHRIST'S DEATH

Much is recorded in the Bible about Jesus' life, teachings, and miracles. However, when He died on the cross, it was for the sins of men. He took our place on the cross so that we might have access to God and to eternal life.

1. *All we like sheep have gone astray; we have turned, every one, to his own way; and <u>the LORD has laid on Him [Christ] the iniquity of us all</u>.* – Isaiah 53:6

2. *(TLB) <u>But it was the Lord's good plan to bruise him and fill him with grief. However, when his soul has been made an offering for sin, then he shall have a multitude of children, many heirs.</u> He shall live again, and God's program shall prosper in his hands. 11 And when he sees all that is accomplished by the anguish of his soul, he shall be satisfied;*

19

and because of what he has experienced, my righteous Servant shall make many to be counted righteous before God, for he shall bear all their sins. 12 Therefore, I will give him the honors of one who is mighty and great because he has poured out his soul unto death. He was counted as a sinner, and he bore the sins of many, and he pled with God for sinners. – Isaiah 53:10-12

3. *For if we have been united together in the likeness of His death, certainly we also shall be in the likeness of His resurrection, 6 knowing this, that our old man was crucified with Him, that the body of sin might be done away with, that we should no longer be slaves of sin. 7 For he who has died has been freed from sin. 8 Now if we died with Christ, we believe that we shall also live with Him, 9 knowing that Christ, having been raised from the dead, dies no more. Death no longer has dominion over Him. 10 For the death that He died, He died to sin once for all; but the life that He lives, He lives to God. 11 Likewise you also, reckon yourselves to be dead indeed to sin, but alive to God in Christ Jesus our Lord. –* Romans 6:5-11

4. (NIV) *He himself bore our sins in his body on the tree, so that we might die to sins and live for righteousness; by his wounds you have been healed. –* 1 Peter 2:24

5. *The blood of Jesus Christ His Son cleanses us from all sin. –* 1 John 1:7

6. *To him who loved us and washed us from our sins in His own blood. –* Revelation 1:5

THE LITERAL RESURRECTION OF JESUS CHRIST FROM THE DEAD

All four of the gospels record not only the literal death but also the literal resurrection of Jesus Christ from the dead. Each author gives the information that was significant to him.

1. *But the angel answered and said to the women, "Do not be afraid, for I know that you seek Jesus who was crucified. 6 He*

is not here; for He is risen, as He said. Come, see the place where the Lord lay. – Matthew 28:5-7

2. *But he said to them, "Do not be alarmed. You seek Jesus of Nazareth, who was crucified. He is risen! He is not here. See the place where they laid Him. – Mark 16:6*

3. *Jesus Himself stood in the midst of them, and said to them . . . Behold My hands and My feet, that it is I Myself. Handle Me and see, for a spirit does not have flesh and bones as you see I have. – Luke 24:36,39*

4. (NIV) *Jesus answered them, 'Destroy this temple, and I will raise it again in three days . . .' But the temple he had spoken of was his body.* John 2:19,21

5. *I lay down My life, that I might take it again. No one takes it from Me, but I lay it down of Myself. I have power to lay it down, and I have power to take it again. – John 10:17-18*

6. *Jesus said to her, "Mary!" She turned and said to Him, "Rabboni!" (which is to say, Teacher). 17 Jesus said to her, "Do not cling to Me, for I have not yet ascended to My Father; but go to My brethren and say to them, 'I am ascending to My Father and your Father, and to My God and your God.'" 18 Mary Magdalene came and told the disciples that she had seen the Lord, and that He had spoken these things to her. – John 20:16-18*

Questions / Considerations:

- The birth, life, death, and resurrection of Jesus were all miraculous. Why do you think that so many miracles were associated with the life of Jesus? How do these set Him apart from other historic religious leaders?

- Why did Jesus have to die for people's sin and how was He able to accomplish it? Consider the idea of substitution, what does that mean in reference to Jesus' death and you personally?

- What hope does Jesus' resurrection offer the world?

THE LITERAL RETURN OF JESUS CHRIST

Jesus Christ is coming again!

1. *Then the sign of the Son of Man will appear in heaven, and then all the tribes of the earth will mourn, and they will see <u>the Son of Man coming on the clouds of heaven with power and great glory</u>. 31 And He will send His angels with a great sound of a trumpet, and they will gather together His elect from the four winds, from one end of heaven to the other.* – Matthew 24:30-31

2. (NIV) *<u>This same Jesus</u>, who has been taken from you into heaven, <u>will come back in the same way</u> you have seen him go into heaven.* Acts 1:11

3. *For this we say to you by the word of the Lord, that we who are alive and remain until the coming of the Lord will by no means precede those who are asleep. 16 <u>For the Lord Himself will descend from heaven</u> with a shout, with the voice of an archangel, and with the trumpet of God. And the dead in Christ will rise first. 17 Then we who are alive and remain shall be caught up together with them in the clouds to meet the Lord in the air. And thus we shall always be with the Lord. 18 Therefore comfort one another with these words.* – 1 Thessalonians 4:15-18

4. (TLB) *Looking forward to that wonderful time we've been expecting, <u>when his glory shall be seen-the glory of our great God and Savior Jesus Christ</u>.* – Titus 2:13

5. *Behold He is coming with clouds, and <u>every eye will see Him</u>, even they who pierced Him.* Revelation 1:7

THE DEITY OF JESUS CHRIST

Jesus came as the Son of God from heaven and became incarnate (in human form).

22

1. *Behold the virgin shall be with child, and bear a Son, and they shall call His name <u>Immanuel,</u>" which is translated, "God <u>with us.</u>" 24 Then Joseph, being aroused from sleep, did as the angel of the Lord commanded him and took to him his wife, 25 and did not know her till she had brought forth her firstborn Son. And he called His name JESUS.* – Matthew 1:23-25

2. NKJV *"In the beginning was the Word, and the Word was with God, and <u>the Word was God</u> . . . <u>And the Word became flesh</u> and dwelt among us, and we beheld His glory, the glory as of the only begotten of the Father, full of grace and truth."* John 1:1,14

3. (NIV) *A week later his disciples were in the house again, and Thomas was with them. Though the doors were locked, Jesus came and stood among them and said, "Peace be with you!" 27 Then he said to Thomas, "Put your finger here; see my hands. Reach out your hand and put it into my side. Stop doubting and believe." 28 <u>Thomas said to him, "My Lord and my God!</u>" 29 Then Jesus told him, "Because you have seen me, you have believed; blessed are those who have not seen and yet have believed." 30 Jesus did many other miraculous signs in the presence of his disciples, which are not recorded in this book. 31 <u>But these are written that you may believe that Jesus is the Christ, the Son of God, and that by believing you may have life in his name</u>* – John 20:26-31

4. *And God said to Moses, "I AM WHO I AM." And He said, "Thus you shall say to the children of Israel, 'I AM has sent me to you.'"* – Exodus 3:14

5. *Jesus said to them, "Most assuredly, I say to you, before Abraham was, I AM."* - John 8:58

6. *God was manifested in the flesh.* – 1 Timothy 3:16

7. *For in Him (Jesus) dwells all the fullness of the Godhead bodily.* – Colossians 2:9

THE TRINITY (NATURE OF GOD)

The word *trinity* is not in the Bible, but from the second century onward Christian theologians adopted it, attempting to explain the nature of God. By the end of the early Church era, leaders from both the western and eastern European churches agreed upon the definition. The Trinity is the doctrine that within the nature of the one God there are three eternal Persons: God the Father, God the Son, and God the Holy Spirit.

The Three Persons of God:

1. *Then God said, Let Us make man in Our image.* – Genesis 1:26

2. *Come, let Us go down and there confuse their language.* – Genesis 11:7

3. (NAS) *And I will pour out on the house of David and on the inhabitants of Jerusalem, the Spirit of grace and of supplication, so that they will look on Me whom they have pierced; and they will mourn for Him, as one mourns for an only son, and they will weep bitterly over Him, like the bitter weeping over a first-born.* – Zechariah 12:10-11

4. (NIV) *As soon as Jesus was baptized, he went up out of the water. At that moment heaven was opened, and he saw the Spirit of God descending like a dove and lighting on him. And a voice from heaven said, 'This is my beloved Son, whom I love; with him I am well pleased."* Matthew 3:16-17

5. (NIV) *Then Jesus came to them and said, "All authority in heaven and on earth has been given to me. 19 Therefore go and make disciples of all nations, baptizing them in the name of the Father and of the Son and of the Holy Spirit, 20 and teaching them to obey everything I have commanded you. And surely I am with you always, to the very end of the age." –* Matthew 28:18-20

The Oneness of God:

1. *Hear, O Israel: the LORD our God, the LORD is one*! - Deuteronomy 6:4

2. *Thus says the LORD, the King of Israel, and his Redeemer the LORD of hosts; I am the First, and I am the Last; besides Me there is no God.* – Isaiah 44:6

3. (NIV) Jesus answered . . . "Anyone who has seen me has seen the Father." - John 14:9

4. One God and Father of all, who is above all, and through all, and in you all. – Ephesians 4:6

5. (NIV) He [Jesus] is the image of the invisible God. – Colossians 1:15

6. (NIV) Ananias, how is it that Satan has so filled your heart that you have lied to the Holy Ghost . . . You have not lied to men but to God. – Acts 5:3-5

Questions / Considerations:

- People try to organize their thoughts and even beliefs. The concept of the Trinity is probably the best definition of the nature of God that exists. Yet, is it really possible for any man to fully comprehend the God who created everything that exists?

SALVATION IS A GIFT THAT COMES THROUGH FAITH IN CHRIST ALONE

Christianity is unique in the idea that salvation is all about faith in the Person of the Lord Jesus Christ. We cannot work for salvation or ever be good enough to gain it by our own merits. It is a gift that is given by God to those who put their faith (trust and belief) in the Lord Jesus Christ and His sacrifice of atonement on our behalf.

1. *Brethren, my heart's desire and prayer to God for Israel is that they may be saved. 2 For I bear them witness that they*

have a zeal for God, but not according to knowledge. 3 For they being ignorant of God's righteousness, and seeking to establish their own righteousness, have not submitted to the righteousness of God. 4 For Christ is the end of the law for righteousness <u>to everyone who believes</u>. – Romans 10:1-4

2. *That if you <u>confess with your mouth the Lord Jesus and believe in your heart</u> that God has raised Him from the dead, you will be saved. 10 For with the heart one believes unto righteousness, and with the mouth confession is made unto salvation.* – Romans 10:9-10

3. *For by grace you have been saved through faith, and that not of yourselves; <u>it is the gift of God, not of works, lest anyone should boast</u>.* – Ephesians 2:8-9

4. *<u>A man is not justified by the works of the law but by the faith of Jesus Christ</u>, even we have believed in Jesus Christ, that we might be justified by the faith in Christ, and not by the works of the law: for by the works of the law no flesh shall be justified.* – Galatians 2:16

THE INSPIRATION OF THE BIBLE

The Bible is the inspired word of God. There is no other book like it in the world. It was written and compiled over 1500 years, on three continents, in three languages, by over forty authors, moved by the Spirit of God to write in unison. It has one continuous theme of redemption from beginning to end. Everyone should read and believe the Bible.

1. *The Spirit of the LORD spoke by me, and His word was on my tongue.* – 2 Samuel 23:2

2. *The grass withers, the flower fades, but the word of our God stands forever.* – Isaiah 40:8

3. *Heaven and earth will pass away, but My words will by no means pass away.* – Matthew 24:35

26

4. (NIV) *Brothers, the Scripture had to be fulfilled which the Holy Spirit spoke long ago through the mouth of David.* – Acts 1:16

5. *Paul, a bondservant of Jesus Christ, called to be an apostle, separated to the gospel of God 2 <u>which He promised before through His prophets in the Holy Scriptures</u>, 3 concerning His Son Jesus Christ our Lord, who was born of the seed of David according to the flesh, 4 and declared to be the Son of God with power according to the Spirit of holiness, by the resurrection from the dead.* – Romans 1:1-4

6. *But you must continue in the things which you have learned and been assured of, knowing from whom you have learned them, 15 and that <u>from childhood you have known the Holy Scriptures, which are able to make you wise for salvation through faith which is in Christ Jesus</u>.* 2 Timothy 3:16

7. *<u>All scripture is given by inspiration of God</u>, and is profitable for doctrine, for reproof, for correction, for instruction in righteousness.* – 2 Timothy 3:16

8. *Knowing this first, that no prophecy of the Scripture is of any private interpretation, for prophecy never came by the will of man, but holy <u>men of God spoke as they were moved by the Holy Spirit</u>.* – 2 Peter 1:20-21

9. *Contend earnestly for the faith which was once for all delivered to the saints.* – Jude 3

10. *He was clothed with a robe dipped in blood, and His name is called The Word of God.* – Revelation 19:13

Questions / Considerations:

- Why do men try to work their way to heaven? Why is faith in Christ the best answer for people and for the world's needs?

- Have you ever felt the Lord speak to you through Scripture? Share a specific experience with the group.

27

3: The Doctrine of Christ

Righteousness will go before Him, and shall make
His footsteps our pathway. – Psalm 85:13

Activity: Consider something that you were taught in life or in school as truth or somehow came to accept it as true, but now you know that it was not true.

THE IMPORTANCE OF WHAT PEOPLE LEARN

The Bible shows us that throughout the history of the world people often learned things that were not true. Many have embraced false doctrines. The word *doctrine* is another name for teachings. People have adhered to and built their lives upon teachings that are not correct. Consider the following passages of Scripture:

1. *A wooden idol is a <u>worthless doctrine</u>* – Jeremiah 10:8

2. *Now when His disciples had come to the other side, they had forgotten to take bread. 6 Then Jesus said to them, "<u>Take heed and beware of the leaven of the Pharisees and the Sadducees</u>." 7 And they reasoned among themselves, saying, "It is because we have taken no bread." 8 But Jesus, being aware of it, said to them, "O you of little faith, why do you reason among yourselves because you have brought no bread? 9 Do you not yet understand, or remember the five loaves of the five thousand and how many baskets you took up? 10 Nor the seven loaves of the four thousand and how many large baskets you took up? 11 How is it you do not understand that I did not speak to you concerning bread? – but to beware of the leaven of the Pharisees and Sadducees." 12 Then they understood that He did not tell them to beware of the leaven of bread, but <u>of the doctrine of the Pharisees and Sadducees</u>.* – Matthew 16: 5-12

3. *For the time will come when* <u>*they will not endure sound*</u>
   <u>*doctrine*</u>*, but according to their own desires, because they*
   have itching ears, they will heap up for themselves teachers; 4
   and they will turn their ears away from the truth, and be turned
   aside to fables. – 2 Timothy 4:3-4

Questions / Considerations:

- Why do you think that Jeremiah referred to a wooden idol as a worthless doctrine? What are possible modern examples of wooden idols?

- What is the purpose of leaven? How does this relate to doctrine?

- Why do people not listen to sound doctrine? Do you know of any examples of modern fables that people adhere to rather than sound doctrine? What about modern religious fables?

THE ROCK AND THE SAND

The Lord Jesus gave an illustration of a life based on wise choices as compared to foolish ones. Consider the following passage:

1. *Therefore whoever hears these sayings of Mine, and does them,*
   I will liken him to a wise man who built his house on the rock:
   25 and the rain descended, the floods came, and the winds
   blew and beat on that house; and it did not fall, for it was
   founded on the rock. 26 "But everyone who hears these
   sayings of Mine, and does not do them, will be like a foolish
   man who built his house on the sand: 27 and the rain
   descended, the floods came, and the winds blew and beat on
   that house; and it fell. And great was its fall. – Matthew 7:24-
   27

Questions / Considerations:

- Both the wise and foolish person heard the instruction of Jesus, so what caused the difference of destiny?

- What do you think the illustrations of rock, sand, house, rain, floods, and wind relate to in our natural and spiritual lives?

THE GOSPEL

The word *gospel* is actually derived from the Anglo-Saxon idea of "the story concerning God". Yet, the Greek counterpart means simply "good news" – the good news about Jesus Christ! It is not only the message about His life, but it has come to be synonymous with the kingdom message of forgiveness of sins and redemption through Christ unto eternal life. The Apostle Paul gives us somewhat of a definition of the gospel in the first passage below, mentions the aspect of grace in the second, and in the other shows that some turn away from it.

1. *Moreover, brethren, I declare to you the gospel which I preached to you, which also you received and in which you stand, 2 by which also you are saved, if you hold fast that word which I preached to you – unless you believed in vain. 3 For I delivered to you first of all that which I also received: that Christ died for our sins according to the Scriptures, 4 and that He was buried, and that He rose again the third day according to the Scriptures, 5 and that He was seen by Cephas, then by the twelve. 6 After that He was seen by over five hundred brethren at once, of whom the greater part remain to the present, but some have fallen asleep. 7 After that He was seen by James, then by all the apostles. 8 Then last of all He was seen by me also, as by one born out of due time.* 1 Corinthians 15:1-8

2. *But none of these things move me; nor do I count my life dear to myself, so that I may finish my race with joy, and the ministry which I received from the Lord Jesus, to testify to the gospel of the grace of God.* – Acts 20:24

3. *I marvel that you are turning away so soon from Him who called you in the grace of Christ, to a different gospel, 7 which is not another; but there are some who trouble you and want to pervert the gospel of Christ.* – Galatians 1:6-7

30

4. (TLB) *I am amazed that you are turning away so soon from God who, in his love and mercy, invited you to share the eternal life he gives through Christ; you are already <u>following a different "way to heaven," which really doesn't go to heaven at all</u>. 7 For there is no other way than the one we showed you; you are being fooled by those who twist and change the truth concerning Christ.* – Galatians 1:6-7

Questions / Considerations:

- Take a moment to ponder on the amazing news that Paul tells us about Christ in 1 Corinthians 15:3-4, and break it down in order to glean the most understanding from it. For instance, how significant is it that Christ actually died? Then consider that He did not just die like all men, but He died for our sins. Why did He have to do that and how could He do that? He died, was buried, and rose on the third day. All of these things were done just as they were prophesied by the prophets of the Old Testament.

- Why would men turn away from the gospel of the grace of God?

THE DOCTRINE OF CHRIST

The doctrine (or teachings) of the Lord Jesus Christ are without parallel in the entire history of the world. Though there have been noble teachers of morality who have insights about God, no one has ever spoken with the authority or had the insight of Jesus because He came as the Son of God. As Christians we ought to pay the utmost attention to those things that Christ taught.

1. *And so it was, when Jesus had ended these sayings, that <u>the people were astonished at His teaching, 29 for He taught them as one having authority,</u> and not as the scribes.* – Matthew 7:28-29

2. *When He had come to His own country, He taught them in their synagogue, so that they were astonished and said,*

"Where did this Man get this wisdom and these mighty works?
– Matthew 13:54

3. *Then He taught them many things by parables, and said to them in His teaching:* - Mark 4:2

4. *But Jesus rebuked him, saying, "Be quiet, and come out of him!" 26 And when the unclean spirit had convulsed him and cried out with a loud voice, he came out of him. 27 Then they were all amazed, so that they questioned among themselves, saying, "What is this? What new doctrine is this? For with authority He commands even the unclean spirits, and they obey Him." 28 And immediately His fame spread throughout all the region around Galilee.* – Mark 1:25-28

5. *Jesus therefore answered and said to them, "Do not murmur among yourselves. 44 No one can come to Me unless the Father who sent Me draws him; and I will raise him up at the last day. 45 It is written in the prophets, 'And they shall all be taught by God.' Therefore, everyone who has heard and learned from the Father comes to Me.* – John 6:43-46

6. *Jesus answered them and said, "My doctrine is not Mine, but His who sent Me. 17 If anyone wills to do His will, he shall know concerning the doctrine, whether it is from God or whether I speak on My own authority. 18 He who speaks from himself seeks his own glory; but He who seeks the glory of the One who sent Him is true, and no unrighteousness is in Him.* – John 7:16-18

7. (NIV) *Jesus answered, "My teaching is not my own. It comes from him who sent me. 17 If anyone chooses to do God's will, he will find out whether my teaching comes from God or whether I speak on my own. 18 He who speaks on his own does so to gain honor for himself, but he who works for the honor of the one who sent him is a man of truth; there is nothing false about him.* – John 7:16-18

Questions / Considerations:

- The people were astonished at Christ's authority, wisdom, miraculous works, and teachings. Yet, not everyone accepted that His doctrine was from God. According to John 7:16-18 what is necessary for people to find out whether the teaching is from God or not?

ABIDING IN THE DOCTRINE OF CHRIST

Near the end of the first century, the Apostle John, as the last surviving apostle, wrote about a group called *Docetists*, who taught that Jesus Christ had not come in the flesh and that His death on the cross must have been an illusion since God could not put on flesh. John instructs those who are in charge of house churches neither to "receive" nor "greet" these "deceivers"; in the sense of greeting them as kindred brothers in Christ, thus giving them freedom in the church to teach their false doctrine. Some today have mistakenly taken this to mean that Christians should be rude to people on the front porch of their personal homes, but we should not; this was referring to house churches and positions of authority in the early Church. One very important thing for us to understand is about the need to abide in "the doctrine of Christ."

1. *For many deceivers have gone out into the world who do not confess Jesus Christ as coming in the flesh. This is a deceiver and an antichrist. 8 Look to yourselves, that we do not lose those things we worked for, but that we may receive a full reward. 9 Whoever transgresses and does not abide in the doctrine of Christ does not have God. He who abides in the doctrine of Christ has both the Father and the Son. 10 If anyone comes to you and does not bring this doctrine, do not receive him into your house nor greet him; 11 for he who greets him shares in his evil deeds. – 2 John 7-11*

2. *(AMP) Anyone who runs on ahead [of God] and does not abide in the doctrine of Christ – who is not content with what He taught – does not have God; but he who continues to live*

in the doctrine (teaching) of Christ – does have God; he has both the Father and the Son. – 2 John 9

Questions / Considerations:

- Why did John consider these people to be deceivers? What were they saying that was not true?

- Why is it important to abide in the teachings that Christ taught us and those correct teachings that are about Christ? The Amplified Version includes the concept of those who are not content. Why is this important?

- Though we should love and not be rude, we should never allow those who do not abide in the doctrine of Christ to speak authoritatively to us about spiritual things.

PRINCIPLES AND DOCTRINES

In lessons four through six, we will be considering the principles of Christ. A principle is fundamental, underlying law, doctrine, or code; it is the underpinning spirit, or the guiding rule which supports its object. The author of Hebrews lists six such principles. These doctrines are derived from Christ's teachings and are primarily about people and how they respond to God.

1. *Therefore leaving the discussion of the elementary principles of Christ, let us go on to perfection, not laying again the foundation of repentance from dead works and of faith toward God, 2 of the doctrine of baptisms, of laying on of hands, of resurrection of the dead, and of eternal judgment.* – Hebrews 6:1-2

2. *(KJV) Therefore leaving the principles of the doctrine of Christ, let us go on unto perfection; not laying again the foundation of repentance from dead works, and of faith toward God, 2 Of the doctrine of baptisms, and of laying on of hands, and of resurrection of the dead, and of eternal judgment.*

34

3. (ASV) *Wherefore leaving <u>the doctrine of the first principles of Christ</u>, let us press on unto perfection; not laying again a foundation of repentance from dead works, and of faith toward God, 2 of the teaching of baptisms, and of laying on of hands, and of resurrection of the dead, and of eternal judgment.*

INSPECTION: THE HISTORIC BELIEFS AND PRINCIPLES OF CHRIST

There is an important difference between the historic Christian beliefs (doctrines) listed in lesson two and the principles (foundational doctrines) listed in lessons four through six. Below they are lined up in two columns:

Historic Christian Beliefs: *Principles of Christ:*

(1) The Virgin Birth of Jesus Christ.   *(1) Repentance from dead works*

(2) The Substitutionary atonement   *(2) Faith towards God*
    of Jesus Christ's death.

(3) The literal resurrection of   *(3) Doctrine of baptisms*
    Jesus Christ from the dead.

(4) The literal return of Jesus Christ   *(4) Laying on of hands*

(5) The deity of Jesus Christ.   *(5) Resurrection of the dead*

(6) The Trinity.   *(6) Eternal Judgment*

(7) Salvation is a gift that comes through
    faith in Jesus Christ alone.

(8) The inspiration of the Bible.

(Doctrines about God)   *(Doctrines about people)*

Notice the distinction between the doctrines listed in both columns. The group in the first column primarily refers to what we believe

35

about Jesus, God and the Bible. The second group is primarily about people, the response to God's invitation, and the future destination of mankind. So, the principles of Christ are about what Christ taught regarding man's salvation, service to God, and the outcome of how we live.

4: The Principles of Christ: Part One

Jesus said to him, "I am the way, the truth, and the life.
No one comes to the Father except through Me. - John 14:6

Activity: A principle is a fundamental, underlying law, doctrine, or code; it is the underpinning spirit, or the guiding rule which supports its object. A principle can be an attitude. What are several positive attitudes that can help someone to become successful in a job or in school.

JESUS IN THE BOOK OF HEBREWS

No one really knows who wrote the Book of Hebrews in the New Testament. Some think it was Paul, others Barnabas, or one of the other apostles. However, its canonical authority and inspiration by God was recognized early on. The powerful theme of the book portrays Jesus Christ as our high priest and intercessor before the throne of God. The new covenant is made possible to us because of His sacrifice and the shedding of His blood for our sins.

1. *Seeing then that <u>we have a great High Priest who has passed through the heavens, Jesus the Son of God</u>, let us hold fast our confession. 15 For we do not have a High Priest who cannot sympathize with our weaknesses, but was in all points tempted as we are, yet without sin. 16 Let us therefore come boldly to the throne of grace, that we may obtain mercy and find grace to help in time of need. – Hebrews 4:14-16*

2. *By so much more Jesus has become a surety of a better covenant. 23 Also there were many priests, because they were prevented by death from continuing. 24 But He, because He continues forever, has an unchangeable priesthood. 25 Therefore He is also able to save to the uttermost those who*

come to God through Him, since <u>He always lives to make</u>
<u>*intercession for them*</u>. – Hebrews 7:22-25

3. (NIV) *He did not enter by means of the blood of goats and calves; but <u>he entered the Most Holy Place once for all by his</u> <u>own blood</u>, having obtained eternal redemption. 13 The blood of goats and bulls and the ashes of a heifer sprinkled on those who are ceremonially unclean sanctify them so that they are outwardly clean. 14 <u>How much more, then, will the blood of</u> <u>Christ, who through the eternal Spirit offered himself</u> <u>unblemished to God, cleanse our consciences from acts that</u> <u>lead to death, so that we may serve the living God!</u> 15 For this reason Christ is the mediator of <u>a new covenant</u>, that those who are called may receive the promised eternal inheritance-now that he has died as a ransom to set them free from the sins committed under the first covenant.* – Hebrews 9:12-15

THE PRINCIPLES OF CHRIST IN HEBREWS

Hebrews 6:1-2 lists six principles. The author implies that these six principles are basic or elementary things that Christians should understand. Based upon what Christ taught, these teachings are essentially about man's salvation, service to God, and the outcome of how we live.

1. *Therefore leaving the discussion of the elementary principles of Christ, let us go on to perfection, <u>not laying again the</u> <u>foundation of repentance from dead works and of faith toward</u> <u>God, 2 of the doctrine of baptisms, of laying on of hands, of</u> <u>resurrection of the dead, and of eternal judgment</u>.* – Hebrews 6:1-2

2. (KJV) *Therefore leaving the principles of the doctrine of Christ, let us go on unto perfection; <u>not laying again the</u> <u>foundation of repentance from dead works, and of faith toward</u> <u>God, 2 Of the doctrine of baptisms, and of laying on of hands,</u> <u>and of resurrection of the dead, and of eternal judgment</u>.* – Hebrews 6:1-2

3. (ASV) *Wherefore leaving the doctrine of the first principles of Christ, let us press on unto perfection;* <u>*not laying again a foundation of repentance from dead works, and of faith toward God, 2 of the teaching of baptisms, and of laying on of hands, and of resurrection of the dead, and of eternal judgment*</u>. – Hebrews 6:1-2

Questions / Considerations:

- What are the six principles (fundamental doctrines) mentioned in this passage?

- Consider the progression of the six principles. How do they progress with respect to a time line? Hint: it begins with repentance.

FOUNDATIONS IN THE BIBLE

Hebrews 6:1 uses the word *foundation* as a symbolic way to represent these principles, once again expressing the idea that these are fundamentally important teachings. Throughout the Bible the importance of foundations is expressed. Here are some examples:

1. **God's throne:** *Righteousness and justice are the <u>foundation</u> of Your throne.* – Psalm 89:14

2. **The earth:** *Where were you when I laid the <u>foundations</u> of the earth?* – Job 38:4

3. **Solomon's temple:** *The <u>foundation</u> was of costly stones, large stones, some ten cubits and some eight cubits.* – 1 Kings 7:10

4. **Rebuilt foundation:** *But many of the priests and Levites and heads of the fathers' houses, old men who had seen the first temple, wept with a loud voice when the <u>foundation</u> of this temple was laid before their eyes. Yet many shouted aloud for joy.* – Ezra 3:12

5. **The righteous:** *Command those who are rich in this present age not to be haughty, nor to trust in uncertain riches but in the living God, who gives us richly all things to enjoy. 18 Let*

39

them do good, that they be rich in good works, ready to give, willing to share, 19 storing up for themselves a good foundation for the time to come, that they may lay hold on eternal life. – 1 Timothy 6:17-19

6. **Responding to God's Word**: *Whoever comes to Me, and hears My sayings and does them, I will show you whom he is like: He is like a man building a house, who dug deep and laid the foundation on the rock. And when the flood arose, the stream beat vehemently against that house, and could not shake it, for it was founded on the rock. 49 But he who heard and did nothing is like a man who built a house on the earth without a foundation, against which the stream beat vehemently; and immediately it fell. And the ruin of that house was great."* - Luke 6:47-49

7. **Ministers of God:** *I have made it my aim to preach the gospel, not where Christ was named, lest I should build on another man's foundation.* – Romans 15:20

8. **Apostles and prophets:** *Now, therefore, you are no longer strangers and foreigners, but fellow citizens with the saints and members of the household of God, 20 having been built on the foundation of the apostles and prophets, Jesus Christ Himself being the chief cornerstone, 21 in whom the whole building, being fitted together, grows into a holy temple in the Lord, 22 in whom you also are being built together for a dwelling place of God in the Spirit.* – Ephesians 2:19-22

9. **Jesus Christ:** *For no other foundation can anyone lay than that which is laid, which is Jesus Christ. 12 Now if anyone builds on this foundation with gold, silver, precious stones, wood, hay, straw, 13 each one's work will become clear; for the Day will declare it, because it will be revealed by fire; and the fire will test each one's work, of what sort it is. 14 If anyone's work which he has built on it endures, he will receive a reward. 15 If anyone's work is burned, he will suffer loss; but he himself will be saved, yet so as through fire.* – 1 Corinthians 3:11-15

Questions / Considerations:

- The idea of these Scriptures is that most, if not all, things have a foundation. Foundations are important to God and essential for Christians. All things that will endure are built on the foundation of Jesus Christ.

- What are some examples that you can think of which represent wood, hay, or stubble? What things would represent gold, silver, precious stones? Are there things in your life (wood, hay, stubble) that you are building with or building on which should change?

ONE: REPENTANCE FROM DEAD WORKS

The first principle (or foundation of doctrine) that is important for the believer is that of repentance from things that do not really please God. It all begins with repentance. The Old Testament idea of repentance was "to sigh", "to turn", or "to return". For example, the people of Nineveh turned from their wicked ways and God spared them. In the New Testament, the idea of repentance often means "to be concerned", "to change the mind", or "to turn towards". In the parable of the prodigal son, we see the young man changing his mind and going back to his father and home (Luke 15:11-32). The basic biblical idea is to turn from death to life in Christ.

Below are biblical examples of the call for repentance:

1. **To Israel:** *Therefore I will judge you, O house of Israel, every one according to his ways," says the Lord GOD. "<u>Repent, and turn from all your transgressions</u>, so that iniquity will not be your ruin. 31 Cast away from you all the transgressions which you have committed, and get yourselves a new heart and a new spirit. For why should you die, O house of Israel? 32 For I have no pleasure in the death of one who dies," says the Lord GOD. "Therefore, turn and live!"* – Ezekiel 18:30-32

2. **Jonah preached repentance:** *Then God saw their works, that <u>they turned from their evil way</u>; and God relented from the*

41

disaster that He had said He would bring upon them, and He did not do it. – Jonah 3:10

3. **John the Baptist preached repentance:** *In those days John the Baptist came preaching in the wilderness of Judea, 2 and saying, "Repent, for the kingdom of heaven is at hand!"* – Matthew 3:1-2

4. **Jesus Christ preached repentance:** *Now after John was put in prison, Jesus came to Galilee, preaching the gospel of the kingdom of God, 15 and saying, "The time is fulfilled, and the kingdom of God is at hand. <u>Repent, and believe in the gospel</u>."* - Mark 1:14-15

5. **Jesus' disciples preached repentance:** *So they went out and preached that people should repent.* – Mark 6:12

6. **Paul preached repentance:** *How I kept back nothing that was helpful, but proclaimed it to you, and taught you publicly and from house to house, 21 testifying to Jews, and also to Greeks, <u>repentance toward God and faith toward our Lord Jesus Christ</u>.* – Acts 20:20-21

7. **To the Gentiles:** *When they heard these things, they became silent; and they glorified God, saying, "Then God has also granted to the Gentiles repentance to life."* – Acts 11:18

8. **God commands it for men everywhere:** (NIV) *In the past God overlooked such ignorance, but now he commands all people everywhere to repent.* – Acts 17:30

9. **God desires all to turn to Him:** (TLB) *He isn't really being slow about his promised return, even though it sometimes seems that way. But he is waiting, for the good reason that he is not willing that any should perish, and he is giving more time for sinners to repent.* – 2 Peter 3:9-10

DEAD WORKS FROM WHICH TO REPENT

Everyone needs to turn to God. That is basic repentance. Yet, there are also works that lead to a dead end from which to turn. It is not the idea that all works are bad. James tells us the importance of proper works (James 2:14-26). Indeed, we should do good works! However, people cannot work to gain eternal life, and there are works of the flesh that lead to death.

1. **Works based upon the Mosaic Law:** *Knowing that a man is not justified by the works of the law but by faith in Jesus Christ, even we have believed in Christ Jesus, that we might be justified by faith in Christ and not by the works of the law; for by the works of the law no flesh shall be justified.* – Galatians 2:16

2. **Works of the flesh:** *Now the works of the flesh are evident, which are: adultery, fornication, uncleanness, lewdness, 20 idolatry, sorcery, hatred, contentions, jealousies, outbursts of wrath, selfish ambitions, dissensions, heresies, 21 envy, murders, drunkenness, revelries, and the like; of which I tell you beforehand, just as I also told you in time past, that those who practice such things will not inherit the kingdom of God.* – Galatians 5:19-21

Questions / Considerations:

- During the years of the early Church, it appears that some were trying to be justified by the works of the Mosaic Law. Do you think that people today try to justify themselves by some set of codes? If so, why do people try to justify themselves?

- Consider the list of the works of the flesh in Galatians' 5:19-21 along with the word *practice* which means to "perform repeatedly or habitually". Notice that the list includes actions, attitudes of the heart, belief systems, and life styles. Why are these called works of the flesh? What does this tell you about the kingdom of God? Just think how wonderful it is when someone repents from any of these things and gives their life to God!

TWO: FAITH TOWARDS GOD

The Bible tells us to repent and believe (to have faith).

1. *Now after John was put in prison, Jesus came to Galilee, preaching the gospel of the kingdom of God, 15 and saying, "The time is fulfilled, and the kingdom of God is at hand. Repent, and believe in the go*spel." – Mark 1:14-15

2. *I kept back nothing that was helpful, but proclaimed it to you, and taught you publicly and from house to house, 21 testifying to Jews, and also to Greeks, repentance toward God and faith toward our Lord Jesus Christ.* – Acts 20:20-22

3. *For they themselves declare concerning us what manner of entry we had to you, and how you turned to God from idols to serve the living and true God, 10 and to wait for His Son from heaven, whom He raised from the dead, even Jesus who delivers us from the wrath to come.* – 1 Thessalonians 1:9-10

IMPORTANCE OF FAITH

Faith is used for every aspect of our relationship with God.

1. **Salvation**: *If you confess with your mouth the Lord Jesus and believe in your heart that God has raised Him from the dead, you will be saved.* – Romans 10:9

2. **Baptism**: *Now if we died with Christ, we believe that we shall also live with Him.* – Romans 6:8

3. **Prayer**: *But let him ask in faith, with no doubting, for he who doubts is like a wave of the sea driven and tossed by the wind.* – James 1:6-7

4. **Giving**: *But this I say: He who sows sparingly will also reap sparingly, and he who sows bountifully will also reap bountifully. 7 So let each one give as he purposes in his heart, not grudgingly or of necessity; for God loves a cheerful giver. 8 And God is able to make all grace abound toward you, that*

you, always having all sufficiency in all things, may have an abundance for every good work. – 2 Corinthians 9:6-9

5. **Healing**: *And the prayer of faith will save the sick, and the Lord will raise him up.* – James 5:15

6. **Communion**: *But let a man examine himself, and so let him eat of the bread and drink of the cup.* – 1 Corinthians 11:28

7. **Deliverance**: *Have mercy on me, O LORD, for I am weak; O LORD, heal me, for my bones are troubled. 3 My soul also is greatly troubled; But You, O LORD -- how long? 4 Return, O LORD, deliver me! Oh, save me for Your mercies' sake!* – Psalm 6:2-4

8. **Provision**: *Seek first the kingdom of God and His righteousness, and all these things shall be added to you.* – Matthew 6:33

9. **Finding God's will:** *Now this is the confidence that we have in Him, that if we ask anything according to His will, He hears us. 15 And if we know that He hears us, whatever we ask, we know that we have the petitions that we have asked of Him.* – 1 John 5:14-15

10. **Christian Lifestyle**: *For we walk by faith, not by sight.* – 2 Corinthians 5:7

Questions / Considerations:

- The apostles asked Jesus to "increase" their faith (Luke 17:6). He answered by telling them about the mustard seed. Seeds grow and so can out faith. Can you think of different ways that our faith can grow? One way is explained in Romans 10:17 about the word of God.

- How can we incorporate faith in a practical way in our daily lives?

5: The Principles of Christ: Part Two

In the way of righteousness is life,
And in its pathway there is no death. – Proverbs 12:28

Activity: Faith towards God is one of the principles of Christ. Faith is a combination of trust and belief. Consider one or more times in your life that you needed to truly have faith towards God. Perhaps it was about direction, health, finances, career, relationships, or other. What were the circumstances and what was the outcome of faith for you?

THE PRINCIPLES OF CHRIST IN HEBREWS

In the last lesson we considered the first two principles: (1) repentance from dead works, and (2) faith toward God. In this lesson we will consider the doctrine of baptisms and of the laying on of hands. This is part of one's response after repentance and faith.

1. *Therefore <u>leaving the discussion</u> of the elementary principles of Christ, <u>let us go on to perfection</u>, not laying again the foundation of repentance from dead works and of faith toward God, 2 <u>of the doctrine of baptisms, of laying on of hands</u>, of resurrection of the dead, and of eternal judgment.* – Hebrews 6:1-2

2. (GWV) *With this in mind, we should stop going over the elementary truths about Christ and <u>move on to topics for more mature people</u>. We shouldn't repeat the basics about turning away from the useless things that we did and the basics about faith in God. 2 We shouldn't repeat the basic teachings about such things as baptisms, setting people apart for holy tasks, dead people coming back to life, and eternal judgment.*

Questions / Considerations:

- The idea of "not laying again" and "go on to perfection" [maturity] indicates that these are basic doctrines which new Christians should understand and move past into more mature doctrines. Do you think most Christians today understand these? Why or why not?

THREE: DOCTRINE OF BAPTISMS

The first striking thing is that this is plural – baptisms. The Greek word *baptizo* means to immerse, to submerge. Consider the following baptisms found in the New Testament:

1. **Baptism of repentance:** *Then Paul said, "John indeed baptized with <u>a baptism of repentance</u>, saying to the people that they should believe on Him who would come after him, that is, on Christ Jesus." –* Acts 19:4

2. **Baptism in water:** *Then Peter answered, 47 <u>"Can anyone forbid water, that these should not be baptized</u> who have received the Holy Spirit just as we have?" 48 And he commanded them to be baptized in the name of the Lord. –* Acts 10:46-48

3. **Baptism in the Holy Spirit:** *I indeed baptize you with water unto repentance, but He who is coming after me is mightier than I, whose sandals I am not worthy to carry. He will <u>baptize you with the Holy Spirit and fire</u>. –* Matthew 3:11

BAPTISM OF REPENTANCE

John the Baptist called people to repent and make ready for the Lord to come. He used water to baptize people. So, at first water baptism was completely associated with the idea of public repentance. Later, repentance from dead works became the first thing that people were to do in coming to the Lord.

1. *John came baptizing in the wilderness and preaching <u>a baptism of repentance for the remission of sins</u>. 5 Then all the land of Judea, and those from Jerusalem, went out to him and*

were all baptized by him in the Jordan River, confessing their sins. – Mark 1:4-5

2. *After John had first preached, before His coming, the baptism of repentance to all the people of Israel. 25 And as John was finishing his course, he said, 'Who do you think I am? I am not He. But behold, there comes One after me, the sandals of whose feet I am not worthy to loose.'* – Acts 13:24-25

BAPTISM IN WATER

The Lord Jesus tells new converts to get baptized in water. Water baptism publicly acknowledges our acceptance of Jesus as Lord and Savior. It changed from the idea of simply representing repentance to the idea of symbolizing Christ's death on our behalf and the newness of resurrection Life.

1. *Go therefore and make disciples of all the nations, baptizing them in the name of the Father and of the Son and of the Holy Spirit.* – Matthew 28:19-20

2. *He who believes and is baptized will be saved; but he who does not believe will be condemned.* – Mark 16:16-17

3. *Then Peter said to them, "Repent, and let every one of you be baptized in the name of Jesus Christ for the remission of sins; and you shall receive the gift of the Holy Spirit.* – Acts 2:38

4. *But when they believed Philip as he preached the things concerning the kingdom of God and the name of Jesus Christ, both men and women were baptized.* – Acts 8:12

5. *Or do you not know that as many of us as were baptized into Christ Jesus were baptized into His death? 4 Therefore we were buried with Him through baptism into death, that just as Christ was raised from the dead by the glory of the Father, even so we also should walk in newness of life. 5 For if we have been united together in the likeness of His death, certainly we also shall be in the likeness of His resurrection, 6 knowing this, that our old man was crucified with Him, that the body of sin might be done away with, that we should no*

48

longer be slaves of sin. 7 For he who has died has been freed from sin. 8 Now if we died with Christ, we believe that we shall also live with Him, 9 knowing that Christ, having been raised from the dead, dies no more. Death no longer has dominion over Him. 10 For the death that He died, He died to sin once for all; but the life that He lives, He lives to God. 11 Likewise you also, reckon yourselves to be dead indeed to sin, but alive to God in Christ Jesus our Lord. – Romans 6:3-11

Questions / Considerations:

- Why do you think that Christ told His followers to get baptized? Why is it important for Christians to really understand it? Why is it significant for people to publicly submit to this?

THE NAME USED IN WATER BAPTISM

From the days of the early Church, both the concept of the Trinity and the name of the Lord Jesus Christ were used for baptismal rites.

1. **Name of the Trinity:** *Go therefore and make disciples of all nations, <u>baptizing them in the name of the Father and of the Son and of the Holy Spirit.</u>* – Matthew 28:19

2. **Name of the Lord:** *And he commanded them to be baptized in <u>the name of the Lord</u>.* – Acts 10:48

3. **Name of Jesus Christ:** *Then Peter said to them, "Repents and let every one of you be baptized in the <u>name of Jesus Christ</u>."* – Acts 2:38

4. **Name of the Lord Jesus:** *They had only been baptized in the <u>name of the Lord Jesus</u>.* – Acts 8:16

5. **Name of Christ Jesus:** *Or do you not know that as many of us as were <u>baptized into Christ Jesus</u> were baptized into His death?* – Romans 6:3

49

Questions / Considerations:

- The different names used are important in that they show that the early Christians were not just looking for a religious formula. They understood the unity, the unique connection, and the direct counter parts between the name of the Lord Jesus Christ and that of the Father, Son, and Holy Spirit.

- Have you been baptized in water? Do you remember the experience? What was important about it for you?

THE TIMING OF THE BAPTISM IN THE HOLY SPIRIT

The baptism of the Holy Spirit is associated with the ideas of being filled with the Holy Spirit and receiving the gift of the Holy Spirit. It can happen in conjunction with water baptism, after water baptism, or even before. Look at the following examples:

1. **In conjunction:** *Then Jesus came from Galilee to John at the Jordan to be baptized by him. 14 And John tried to prevent Him, saying, "I need to be baptized by You, and are You coming to me?" 15 But Jesus answered and said to him, "Permit it to be so now, for thus it is fitting for us to fulfill all righteousness." Then he allowed Him. 16 When He had been baptized, Jesus came up immediately from the water; and behold, the heavens were opened to Him, and He saw the Spirit of God descending like a dove and alighting upon Him. 17 And suddenly a voice came from heaven, saying, "This is My beloved Son, in whom I am well pleased."* – Matthew 3:13-17

2. **After:** *Now when the apostles who were at Jerusalem heard that Samaria had received the word of God, they sent Peter and John to them, 15 who, when they had come down, prayed for them that they might receive the Holy Spirit. 16 For as yet He had fallen upon none of them. They had only been baptized in the name of the Lord Jesus. 17 Then they laid hands on them, and they received the Holy Spirit.* – Acts 8:14-17

3. **Before:** *While Peter was still speaking these words, the Holy Spirit fell upon all those who heard the word. 45 And those of the circumcision who believed were astonished, as many as came with Peter, because the gift of the Holy Spirit had been poured out on the Gentiles also. 46 For they heard them speak with tongues and magnify God. Then Peter answered, 47 "Can anyone forbid water, that these should not be baptized who have received the Holy Spirit just as we have?" 48 And he commanded them to be baptized in the name of the Lord.* – Acts 10:44-48

Questions / Considerations:

- The first passage above shows us Jesus fulfilling all righteousness. In what way was He fulfilling it in this situation? Can you think of other ways that He fulfilled it?

- What are some things that the differences in the timing of the reception of the Holy Spirit in the passages above suggest to us about God?

WHO BAPTIZES US IN THE HOLY SPIRIT?

The Lord Jesus Christ baptizes (immerses) us in the Holy Spirit.

1. *I indeed baptized you with water, but He will baptize you with the Holy Spirit.* – Mark 1:8

2. *John answered, saying to all, "I indeed baptized you with water, but One mightier than I is coming, whose sandal strap I am not worthy to loose. He will baptize you with the Holy Spirit and with fire." His winnowing fan is in His hand, and He will thoroughly clean out His threshing floor, and gather the wheat into His barn; but the chaff He will burn with unquenchable fire."* – Luke 3:16-17

Questions / Considerations:

- Consider the idea of fire in the second passage. It appears to be in reference to burning up chaff. Does

51

this refer to Christians? If so, how? Is there anything that needs to be burned up in your life?

THE GIFTS AND FRUIT ASSOCIATIATED WITH THE HOLY SPIRIT

It is not possible to mention all of the amazing things that the Holy Spirit provides for us, but here are some.

1. **Speaking in other tongues:** *Then there appeared to them divided tongues, as of fire, and one sat upon each of them. 4 And they were all filled with the Holy Spirit and began to speak with other tongues, as the Spirit gave them utterance.* – Acts 2:3-4

2. **Diversities of gifts:** *There are diversities of gifts, but the same Spirit. 5 There are differences of ministries, but the same Lord. 6 And there are diversities of activities, but it is the same God who works all in all. 7 But the manifestation of the Spirit is given to each one for the profit of all: 8 for to one is given the word of wisdom through the Spirit, to another the word of knowledge through the same Spirit, 9 to another faith by the same Spirit, to another gifts of healings by the same Spirit, 10 to another the working of miracles, to another prophecy, to another discerning of spirits, to another different kinds of tongues, to another the interpretation of tongues. 11 But one and the same Spirit works all these things, distributing to each one individually as He wills.* – 1 Corinthians 12:4-11

3. **Fruit of the Spirit:** *But the fruit of the Spirit is love, joy, peace, longsuffering, kindness, goodness, faithfulness, 23 gentleness, self-control. Against such there is no law.* – Galatians 5:22-23

Questions / Considerations:

- Consider the gifts of the Holy Spirit. What are some that you have seen used by Christians? All of them are supernatural, but are there any that seem to be more commonly manifested than others? The words "other tongues" refers to different languages given by supernatural means. Can a person speak in more than one tongue?

- Notice that the word *fruit* is singular. So, if someone has received the Holy Spirit, should that individual grow all of this fruit?

FOUR: LAYING ON OF HANDS

Throughout Scripture, the laying on of hands is used for numerous things: blessing, confession, healing, anointing; imparting gifts, strength, guidance, and confirmation.

1. **Blessing:** (TLB) *But Israel crossed his arms as he stretched them out <u>to lay his hands upon the boys' heads</u>, so that his right hand was upon the head of Ephraim, the younger boy, and his left hand was upon the head of Manasseh, the older. He did this purposely.* – Genesis 48:14

2. **Old covenant confession of sin:** *Then <u>he shall put his hand on the head of the burnt offering</u>, and it will be accepted on his behalf to make atonement for him.* – Leviticus 1:4

3. **Healing:** (NIV) *Then one of the synagogue rulers, named Jairus, came there. Seeing Jesus, he fell at his feet 23 and pleaded earnestly with him, "My little daughter is dying. <u>Please come and put your hands on her so that she will be healed and live</u>." 24 So Jesus went with him.* – Mark 5:21-24

4. **Gifts:** *Therefore I remind you to stir up <u>the gift of God which is in you through the laying on of my hands</u>. For God has not given us a spirit of fear, but of power and of love and of a sound mind.* – 2 Timothy 1:6-7

5. **Confirmation:** *And the saying pleased the whole multitude. And they chose Stephen, a man full of faith and the Holy Spirit, and Philip, Prochorus, Nicanor, Timon, Parmenas, and Nicolas, a proselyte from Antioch, 6 whom they set before the apostles; and <u>when they had prayed, they laid hands on them</u>.* – Acts 6:5-6

6. **Prayer:** *Then little children were brought to Him that He might put His hands on them and pray, but the disciples rebuked them. 14 But Jesus said, "Let the little children come to Me, and do not forbid them; for of such is the kingdom of heaven." 15 And He laid His hands on them and departed from there.* – Matthew 19:13-15

7. **Signs and wonders**: *And through the hands of the apostles many signs and wonders were done among the people.* – Acts 5:12

Questions / Considerations:

- Why do you think that the Lord has people use hands in such a way as described above?

- How have you personally seen the laying on of hands used in Christian life?

6: The Principles of Christ: Part Three

Was it not You who dried up the sea, the waters of the great deep;
Who made the depths of the sea a pathway for the redeemed to cross
over?
– Isaiah 51:10 (NASU)

Activity: We are so blessed to be in a living, growing relationship
with the Lord Jesus. He loves us and has wonderful plans for each of
His followers. Yet, we also have the privilege of making goals,
creating strategies, and doing things in our lives that bless Him. What
are three things that you would like to do in your life for God or
because of your relationship with God, which you have not yet done?

THE PRINCIPLES OF CHRIST IN HEBREWS

In the last two lessons we considered the first four principles: (1)
repentance from dead works, (2) faith toward God, (3) doctrine of
baptisms, and (4) the laying on of hands. In this lesson we will
consider the final two: resurrection of the dead and eternal judgment.
All of these doctrines are primarily about people and how they
respond to God. Remember that the historic Christian beliefs that we
considered in lesson three are primarily about God and the Bible.

1. *Therefore leaving the discussion of the elementary principles
   of Christ, let us go on to perfection, not laying again the
   foundation of repentance from dead works and of faith toward
   God, 2 of the doctrine of baptisms, of laying on of hands, of
   resurrection of the dead, and of eternal judgment.* – Hebrews
   6:1-2

2. (NIV) *Therefore let us leave the elementary teachings about
   Christ and go on to maturity, not laying again the foundation
   of repentance from acts that lead to death, and of faith in God,*

2 instruction about baptisms, the laying on of hands, the resurrection of the dead, and eternal judgment.

3. (TLB) *Let us stop going over the same old ground again and again, always teaching those first lessons about Christ. Let us go on instead to other things and become mature in our understanding, as strong Christians ought to be. Surely we don't need to speak further about the foolishness of trying to be saved by being good, or about the necessity of faith in God; 2 you don't need further instruction about baptism and spiritual gifts and the resurrection of the dead and eternal judgment.*

FIVE: RESURRECTION OF THE DEAD

The Bible tells us of three resurrections. Belief in all of these is important to the believer.

1. **The resurrection of Jesus Christ:** *But the angel answered and said to the women, "Do not be afraid, for I know that you seek Jesus who was crucified. 6 He is not here; for He is risen, as He said. Come, see the place where the Lord lay.* – Matthew 28:5-7

2. **The spiritual resurrection of the believer:** *Therefore we were buried with Him through baptism into death, that just as Christ was raised from the dead by the glory of the Father, even so we also should walk in newness of life. 5 For if we have been united together in the likeness of His death, certainly we also shall be in the likeness of His resurrection, 6 knowing this, that our old man was crucified with Him, that the body of sin might be done away with, that we should no longer be slaves of sin.* – Romans 6:4-6

3. **The ultimate resurrection of the dead:** *Do not marvel at this; for the hour is coming in which all who are in the graves will hear His voice 29 and come forth -- those who have done good, to the resurrection of life, and those who have done evil, to the resurrection of condemnation.* – John 5:28-30

THE RESURRECTION OF JESUS CHRIST

This doctrine was also considered in lesson three under historic Christian beliefs. Here are some additional important aspects of it.

1. **Jesus predicted His resurrection:** *From that time Jesus began to show to His disciples that He must go to Jerusalem, and suffer many things from the elders and chief priests and scribes, and be killed, and be raised the third day. – Matthew 16:21*

2. **He was resurrected in the same body:** *Now as they said these things, Jesus Himself stood in the midst of them, and said to them, "Peace to you." 37 But they were terrified and frightened, and supposed they had seen a spirit. 38 And He said to them, "Why are you troubled? And why do doubts arise in your hearts? 39 Behold My hands and My feet, that it is I Myself. Handle Me and see, for a spirit does not have flesh and bones as you see I have." 40 When He had said this, He showed them His hands and His feet. 41 But while they still did not believe for joy, and marveled, He said to them, "Have you any food here?" 42 So they gave Him a piece of a broiled fish and some honeycomb. 43 And He took it and ate in their presence. – Luke 24:36-43*

3. **He was seen by many witnesses:** *For I delivered to you first of all that which I also received: that Christ died for our sins according to the Scriptures, 4 and that He was buried, and that He rose again the third day according to the Scriptures, 5 and that He was seen by Cephas, then by the twelve. 6 After that He was seen by over five hundred brethren at once, of whom the greater part remain to the present, but some have fallen asleep. 7 After that He was seen by James, then by all the apostles. 8 Then last of all He was seen by me also, as by one born out of due time. – 1 Corinthians 15:3-8*

Questions / Considerations:

- The Corinthians account does not mention the very first person who saw Jesus after His resurrection, but

57

each of the four gospels mentions her. It wasn't one of the apostles. Who was it? See Matthew 28:1.

- Jesus told the disciples several times that He would be killed and then be raised from the dead on the third day. Why do you think it was so hard for them to understand and then to believe it when it happened? How do you think that you would have responded?

- Notice that James the brother of Jesus got a special visit after the resurrection (1 Corinthians 15:7). Yet, according to John 7:5 he was an unbeliever beforehand. Wow, can you imagine what happened in that meeting! Also, see Acts 1:14.

THE SPIRITUAL RESURRECTION OF THE BELIEVER

Our faith in Jesus Christ, in what He did for us, and in His resurrection, brings us into newness of life.

1. **It brings salvation:** *If you confess with your mouth the Lord Jesus and* <u>*believe in your heart that God has raised Him from the dead, you will be saved*</u>*. 10 For with the heart one believes unto righteousness, and with the mouth confession is made unto salvation.* – Romans 10:9-10

2. **It makes us dead to sin but alive to Christ:** *Now if we died with Christ, we believe that we shall also live with Him, 9 knowing that Christ, having been raised from the dead, dies no more. Death no longer has dominion over Him. 10 For the death that He died, He died to sin once for all; but the life that He lives, He lives to God. 11* <u>*Likewise you also, reckon yourselves to be dead indeed to sin, but alive to God in Christ Jesus our Lord*</u>. – Romans 6:8-11

3. **It brings forgiveness and overcomes sins:** (TLB) *For in baptism you see how your old, evil nature died with him and was buried with him; and then you came up out of death with him into a new life because you trusted the Word of the mighty God who raised Christ from the dead. 13 You were dead in*

58

sins, and your sinful desires were not yet cut away. <u>Then he gave you a share in the very life of Christ, for he forgave all your sins</u>, 14 and blotted out the charges proved against you, the list of his commandments which you had not obeyed. He took this list of sins and destroyed it by nailing it to Christ's cross. <u>15 In this way God took away Satan's power to accuse you of sin, and God openly displayed to the whole world Christ's triumph at the cross where your sins were all taken away</u>. – Colossians 2:12-15

4. **It produces justification:** *Now it was not written for his sake alone that it was imputed to him, 24 but also for us. It shall be imputed to us who believe in Him who raised up Jesus our Lord from the dead, 25 who was delivered up because of our offenses, and <u>was raised because of our justification</u>.* – Romans 4:23-25

5. **It brings life to our mortal bodies:** *But if the Spirit of Him who raised Jesus from the dead dwells in you, He who raised Christ from the dead will also <u>give life to your mortal bodies through His Spirit who dwells in you</u>.* – Romans 8:11

6. **It prepares us for the resurrection of all from the graves:** *Jesus said to her, "I am the resurrection and the life. <u>He who believes in Me, though he may die, he shall live</u>. 26 And whoever lives and believes in Me shall never die. Do you believe this?"* - John 11:25-26

Questions / Considerations:

- Why do you think it is important for Christians to believe that Jesus Christ was raised from the dead?

- What did Christ's death and resurrection do to our sins and Satan's power to accuse us?

- How does faith in Jesus prepare us for the future resurrection of all from the graves?

THE ULTIMATE RESURRECTION OF THE DEAD

The word *sleep* is also used in Scripture to describe the dead. Though there are mysteries surrounding the ultimate resurrection, and though theologians debate about the sequence and timing of end time events, the Bible assures us that an ultimate resurrection will occur.

1. (NIV) But Christ has indeed been raised from the dead, the first fruits of those who have fallen asleep. 21 For since death came through a man, the resurrection of the dead comes also through a man. 22 For as in Adam all die, so in Christ all will be made alive. 23 But each in his own turn: Christ, the first fruits; then, when he comes, those who belong to him. 24 Then the end will come, when he hands over the kingdom to God the Father after he has destroyed all dominion, authority and power. – 1 Corinthians 15:20-25

2. For the Lord Himself will descend from heaven with a shout, with the voice of an archangel, and with the trumpet of God. And the dead in Christ will rise first. – 1 Thessalonians 4:16-17

3. *Behold, I tell you a mystery: We shall not all sleep, but we shall all be changed -- 52 in a moment, in the twinkling of an eye, at the last trumpet. For the trumpet will sound, and the dead will be raised incorruptible, and we shall be changed. 53 For this corruptible must put on incorruption, and this mortal must put on immortality.* – 1 Corinthians 15:51-53

4. *And many of those who sleep in the dust of the earth shall awake, some to everlasting life, some to shame and everlasting contempt. 3 Those who are wise shall shine like the brightness of the firmament, and those who turn many to righteousness like the stars forever and ever.* – Daniel 12:2-3

5. (NIV) *Do not be amazed at this, for a time is coming when all who are in their graves will hear his voice 29 and come out- those who have done good will rise to live, and those who have done evil will rise to be condemned. 30 By myself I can do*

nothing; I judge only as I hear, and my judgment is just, for I seek not to please myself but him who sent me. – John 5:28-30

Questions / Considerations:

- The Bible makes it plain that there will be a literal resurrection. What does this mean for you and for all of mankind?

- Based on this truth, how should we live our lives now? How should we face the minor daily problems? How should we treat others?

SIX: ETERNAL JUDGMENT

Everyone will come before the judgment seat of Christ.

1. *But why do you judge your brother? Or why do you show contempt for your brother? For <u>we shall all stand before the judgment seat of Christ.</u> 11 For it is written: "As I live, says the LORD, every knee shall bow to Me, and every tongue shall confess to God." 12 So then each of us shall give account of himself to God. 13 Therefore let us not judge one another anymore, but rather resolve this, not to put a stumbling block or a cause to fall in our brother's way.* - Romans 14:10-13

2. *Therefore we make it our aim, whether present or absent, to be well pleasing to Him. 10 for <u>we must all appear before the judgment seat of Christ,</u> that each one may receive the things done in the body, according to what he has done, whether good or bad.* 2 Corinthians 5:9-11

3. *I charge you therefore before God and <u>the Lord Jesus Christ, who will judge the living and the dead at His appearing and His kingdom.</u>* – 2 Timothy 4:1-2

4. *They will give an account to <u>Him who is ready to judge the living and the dead.</u> 6 for this reason the gospel was preached also to those who are dead, that they might be judged according to men in the flesh, but live according to God in the spirit.* – 1 Peter 4:5-6

5. *When the Son of Man comes in His glory, and all the holy angels with Him, then He will sit on the throne of His glory. 32 All the nations will be gathered before Him, and He will separate them one from another, as a shepherd divides his sheep from the goats. 33 And He will set the sheep on His right hand, but the goats on the left.* – Matthew 25:31-34

6. *Finally, there is laid up for me the crown of righteousness, which the Lord, the righteous Judge, will give to me on that Day, and not to me only but also to all who have loved His appearing.* – 2 Timothy 4:8

Questions / Considerations:

- According to these passages, who will be the judge? Who will be judged? Upon what will the judgment be based?

- How does the passage in Matthew symbolize the difference between the two groups? What will all who have loved His appearing receive?

WHAT PRINCIPLES GOVERN GOD'S JUDGMENT?

The Bible makes us aware of some of the principles by which people will be judged.

1. **By our belief in Jesus Christ:** *For God so loved the world that He gave His only begotten Son, that whoever believes in Him should not perish by have everlasting life.* – John 3:16

2. **By the witness of others:** *The men of Nineveh will rise up in the judgment with this generation and condemn it, because they repented at the preaching of Jonah; and indeed a greater than Jonah is here. 42 The queen of the South will rise up in the judgment with this generation and condemn it, for she came from the ends of the earth to hear the wisdom of Solomon; and indeed a greater than Solomon is here.* – Matthew 12:41-42

3. **By the light of Christ:** (TLB) *Their sentence is based on this fact: that the Light from heaven came into the world, but they loved the darkness more than the Light, for their deeds were evil. 20* <u>*They hated the heavenly Light*</u> *because they wanted to sin in the darkness. They stayed away from that Light for fear their sins would be exposed and they would be punished. 21* <u>*But those doing right come gladly to the Light*</u> *to let everyone see that they are doing what God wants them to.* – John 3:19-21

4. **By obedience to God's law in the heart:** (NIV) *For it is not those who hear the law who are righteous in God's sight, but it is those who obey the law who will be declared righteous. 14(Indeed, when Gentiles, who do not have the law, do by nature things required by the law, they are a law for themselves, even though they do not have the law, 15 since they show that the requirements of the law are written on their hearts, their consciences also bearing witness, and their thoughts now accusing, now even defending them.) 16* <u>*This will take place on the day when God will judge men's secrets through Jesus Christ*</u>*, as my gospel declares.* – Romans 2:13-16

5. **By the Word of God:** *He who rejects Me, and does not receive My words, has that which judges him --* <u>*the word that I have spoken will judge him in the last day.*</u> *49 For I have not spoken on My own authority; but the Father who sent Me gave Me a command, what I should say and what I should speak. 50 And I know that His command is everlasting life. Therefore, whatever I speak, just as the Father has told Me, so I speak."* – John 12:48-50

6. **By the person's works:** *And I saw the dead, small and great, standing before God, and books were opened. And another book was opened, which is the Book of Life. And* <u>*the dead were judged according to their works*</u>*, by the things which were written in the books. 13 The sea gave up the dead who were in it, and Death and Hades delivered up the dead who were in them. And they were judged, each one according to his works. 14 Then Death and Hades were cast into the lake of fire. This*

is the second death.   15 And anyone not found written in the Book of Life was cast into the lake of fire. – Revelation 20:12-15

7. **By the person's words:** (TLB) *And I tell you this, that you must give account on Judgment Day for every idle word you speak. 37 Your words now reflect your fate then: either you will be justified by them or you will be condemned.* – Matthew 12:36-37

REWARDS OF THE RIGHTEOUS

We are made righteous through the righteousness of Jesus Christ. The rewards that await Christ's followers in eternal life are more than can be listed; here are some.

1. *I saw a new heaven and a new earth, for the first heaven and the first earth had passed away. And there was no more sea.* – Revelation 21:1

2. *And God will wipe away every tear from their eyes; there shall be no more death, nor sorrow, nor crying. There shall be no more pain, for the former things have passed away. 5 Then He who sat on the throne said, "Behold, I make all things new." And He said to me, "Write, for these words are true and faithful." 6 And He said to me, "It is done! I am the Alpha and the Omega, the Beginning and the End. I will give of the fountain of the water of life freely to him who thirsts. 7 He who overcomes shall inherit all things, and I will be his God and he shall be My son.* – Revelation 21:4-7

3. *And he showed me a pure river of water of life, clear as crystal, proceeding from the throne of God and of the Lamb. 2 In the middle of its street, and on either side of the river, was the tree of life, which bore twelve fruits, each tree yielding its fruit every month. The leaves of the tree were for the healing of the nations. 3 And there shall be no more curse, but the throne of God and of the Lamb shall be in it, and His servants shall serve Him. 4 They shall see His face, and His name shall be on their foreheads. 5 There shall be no night there: They need no lamp*

nor light of the sun, for the Lord God gives them light. And they shall reign forever and ever. – Revelation 22:1-5

4. *You will show me the path of life; in Your presence is fullness of joy; at your right hand are pleasures forevermore*. – Psalms 16:11

Questions / Considerations:

- Take a moment and give thanks to the Lord for what He has done in your life. Consider the blessings that await the followers of Christ. Which ones stand out to you? Ponder how these will be possible. What do you think the new earth and new heaven might be like at that time?

7: Everyday Christian Living: Part One

I have taught you in the way of wisdom;
I have led you in right paths. – Proverbs 4:11

Activity: Everyone has learned from a mistake, by experience, or has done something that if they could do it over would change how it was done or what was done. We also learn from the example of others. Share about something specific in your life that you would do again differently if given the opportunity, or share about something that you saw someone else do that you would have done differently. This can be recent or from years ago.

Note: In this lesson and the next, we will consider living as Christians in this world. We certainly learn by experience and by the example of others. As Christians, we also have the valuable resource of the Bible that we have been learning from in these lessons. What advice does the Bible give us about living every day and preparing for the future?

THE IMPORTANCE OF WISDOM

One important thing for Christians to learn about is wisdom, gaining, it, growing in it, and utilizing it. The word wisdom and other words associated with it are used hundreds of times in the Bible. Wisdom is ascribed to many biblical characters. The biblical concepts of wisdom, understanding, and knowledge can be described in different ways. One approach is that they are comparable. The terms appear to be easily exchanged because they are part of each other or build together. A different approach is that there is a hierarchy: knowledge, understanding, wisdom. Knowledge is the facts. Understanding is the ability to categorize and group those facts appropriately. Wisdom is the ability to use or apply those categories of facts in the right way. So, it is most important. The book of *Proverbs* records dozens of passages about wisdom. Here are a few.

1. *My son, if you receive my words, and treasure my commands within you, 2 so that you <u>incline your ear to wisdom</u>, and apply your heart to understanding.* – Proverbs 2:1-2

2. *For <u>the LORD gives wisdom</u>; from His mouth come knowledge and understanding; 7 <u>He stores up sound wisdom</u> for the upright; He is a shield to those who walk uprightly.* – Proverbs 2:6-7

3. *<u>Happy is the man who finds wisdom</u>, And the man who gains understanding.* – Proverbs 3:13

4. (TLB) *<u>Getting wisdom is the most important thing</u> you can do! And with your wisdom, <u>develop common sense and good judgment</u>. 8 If you exalt wisdom, she will exalt you. Hold her fast, and she will lead you to great honor; she will place a beautiful crown upon your head.* – Proverbs 4:7-10

5. (NIV) *<u>The fear of the LORD is the beginning of wisdom</u>, and knowledge of the Holy One is understanding.* – Proverbs 9:10

6. *<u>Through wisdom a house is built</u>, and by understanding it is established; 4 by knowledge the rooms are filled with all precious and pleasant riches.* – Proverbs 24:3-4

LEARNING ABOUT WISDOM FROM THE LORD JESUS

Jesus was wise and made it part of His ministry and instruction.

1. **He was filled with wisdom:** *And the Child grew and became strong in spirit, <u>filled with wisdom</u>; and the grace of God was upon Him.* – Luke 2:40

2. **He grew in wisdom:** *Then He went down with them and came to Nazareth, and was subject to them, but His mother kept all these things in her heart. 52 And Jesus <u>increased in wisdom</u> and stature, and in favor with God and men.* – Luke 2:51-52

3. **Astonished people with His wisdom:** *Then He went out from there and came to His own country, and His disciples followed*

Him. 2 And when the Sabbath had come, He began to teach in the synagogue. And many hearing Him were astonished, saying, "Where did this Man get these things? And <u>what wisdom is this which is given to Him</u>, that such mighty works are performed by His hands! – Mark 6:1-3

4. **Justified the actions of God's servants:** *For John the Baptist came neither eating bread nor drinking wine, and you say, 'He has a demon.' 34 The Son of Man has come eating and drinking, and you say, 'Look, a glutton and a winebibber, a friend of tax collectors and sinners!' 35 <u>But wisdom is justified by all her children</u>.* - Luke 7:33-35

5. **He exhorts those not taking heed:** *The queen of the South will rise up in the judgment with this generation and condemn it, for she came from the ends of the earth to hear the wisdom of Solomon; and indeed <u>a greater than Solomon is here</u>.* – Matthew 12:42

6. **He describes His followers:** (TLB) *<u>All who listen to my instructions and follow them are wise</u>, like a man who builds his house on solid rock. 25 Though the rain comes in torrents, and the floods rise and the storm winds beat against his house, it won't collapse, for it is built on rock.* – Matthew 7:24-25

7. **He admonishes those He sends out:** *Behold, I send you out as sheep in the midst of wolves. Therefore, <u>be wise as serpents</u> and harmless as doves.* – Matthew 10:16-17

8. **The parable of the faithful servant:** *<u>Who then is a faithful and wise servant</u>, whom his master made ruler over his household, to give them food in due season? 46 Blessed is that servant whom his master, when he comes, will find so doing. 47 Assuredly, I say to you that he will make him ruler over all his goods.* – Matthew 24:45-47

9. **The parable of the ten virgins:** *Then the kingdom of heaven shall be likened to ten virgins who took their lamps and went out to meet the bridegroom. 2 Now <u>five of them were wise</u>, and five were foolish. 3 Those who were foolish took their*

lamps and took no oil with them, 4 but <u>the wise took oil in their</u>
<u>vessels with their lamps</u>. 5 But while the bridegroom was
delayed, they all slumbered and slept. 6 "And at midnight a
cry was heard: 'Behold, the bridegroom is coming; go out to
meet him!' 7 Then all those virgins arose and trimmed their
lamps. 8 And the foolish said to the wise, 'Give us some of
your oil, for our lamps are going out.' 9 <u>But the wise answered,</u>
<u>saying, 'No, lest there should not be enough for us and you;</u>
<u>but go rather to those who sell, and buy for yourselves.' 10</u>
<u>And while they went to buy, the bridegroom came, and those</u>
<u>who were ready went in with him to the wedding; and the door</u>
<u>was shut.</u> 11 "Afterward the other virgins came also, saying,
'Lord, Lord, open to us!' 12 But he answered and said,
'Assuredly, I say to you, I do not know you.' 13 "Watch
therefore, for you know neither the day nor the hour in which
the Son of Man is coming. Matthew 25:1-13

Questions / Considerations:

- If Jesus could increase in wisdom, so can we. Yet, it also says that he grew in favor with God and man. Do you think there is a connection between growing in wisdom and gaining favor?

- Why are they called wise that hear and follow Jesus' instructions?

- What do you think He means by "wise as serpents"?

- Why do you think the servant is called faithful and wise? What do you think the oil in the virgins' vessels symbolizes? Light, Holy Spirit, other?

HEAVENLY WISDOM

The Bible distinguishes between true heavenly wisdom and other so-called wisdom.

1. *However, we speak wisdom among those who are mature, yet not the wisdom of this age, nor of the rulers of this age, who are coming to nothing. 7 But we speak the wisdom of God in a mystery, the hidden wisdom which God ordained before the ages for our glory, 8 which none of the rulers of this age knew; for had they known, they would not have crucified the Lord of glory.* – 1 Corinthians 2:6-8

2. (NIV) *Do not deceive yourselves. If any one of you thinks he is wise by the standards of this age, he should become a "fool" so that he may become wise. 19 For the wisdom of this world is foolishness in God's sight. As it is written: "He catches the wise in their craftiness"; 20 and again, "The Lord knows that the thoughts of the wise are futile."* – 1 Corinthians 3:18-20

3. (TLB) *If you are wise, live a life of steady goodness so that only good deeds will pour forth. And if you don't brag about them, then you will be truly wise! 14 And by all means don't brag about being wise and good if you are bitter and jealous and selfish; that is the worst sort of lie. 15 For jealousy and selfishness are not God's kind of wisdom. Such things are earthly, unspiritual, inspired by the devil. 16 For wherever there is jealousy or selfish ambition, there will be disorder and every other kind of evil. 17 But the wisdom that comes from heaven is first of all pure and full of quiet gentleness. Then it is peace-loving and courteous. It allows discussion and is willing to yield to others; it is full of mercy and good deeds. It is wholehearted and straightforward and sincere. 18 And those who are peacemakers will plant seeds of peace and reap a harvest of goodness.* – James 3:13-18

Questions / Considerations:

- Why do you think the apostle Paul in the letter to the Corinthians tells them that "the wisdom of this world is foolishness in God's sight"?

- One of the attributes of heavenly wisdom in *James* is that it is peace-loving. What are the other attributes?

What are the things that can accompany earthly wisdom?

PRAYING TO GOD FOR WISDOM

We have the privilege and right to seek God for wisdom.

1. **Praying with persistence:** *Ask, and it will be given to you; seek, and you will find; knock, and it will be opened to you. 8 For everyone who asks receives, and he who seeks finds, and to him who knocks it will be opened. 9 Or what man is there among you who, if his son asks for bread, will give him a stone? 10 Or if he asks for a fish, will he give him a serpent? 11 If you then, being evil, know how to give good gifts to your children, how much more will your Father who is in heaven give good things to those who ask Him*! - Matthew 7:7-12

2. **Praying with faith:** *If any of you lacks wisdom, let him ask of God, who gives to all liberally and without reproach, and it will be given to him. 6 But let him ask in faith, with no doubting, for he who doubts is like a wave of the sea driven and tossed by the wind. 7 For let not that man suppose that he will receive anything from the Lord; 8 he is a double-minded man, unstable in all his ways.* – James 1:5-8

3. **Praying for others:** *For this reason we also, since the day we heard it, do not cease to pray for you, and to ask that you may be filled with the knowledge of His will in all wisdom and spiritual understanding; 10 that you may walk worthy of the Lord, fully pleasing Him, being fruitful in every good work and increasing in the knowledge of God.* – Colossians 1:9-11

Questions / Considerations:

- Can we expect to receive good gifts from our heavenly Father? Why?

- When it comes to seeking wisdom from God, why is it important that we ask with faith?

- How often do we stop and ask God to bless others with knowledge, understanding, and wisdom?

PRAYER POWER

The Bible has much to say about the subject of prayer. Many books have been written about it. A disciple once asked Jesus to teach them to pray (Luke 11:1), and He responded with the example of the Lord's Prayer (Luke 11:2-4). There are many prayers in both the Old and New Testaments. The Patriarchs often prayed. Many of the *Psalms* by David include prayers. Jesus often went up into the mountains to be alone to pray. Prayer can be done alone or in groups. Prayer is one of the most important things that Christians do because it is how we communicate with God. Prayer can bring sweet communion with God. It is often a two-way communication. God answers prayer and sometimes those answers are quite powerful.

1. *And she said, "O my lord! As your soul lives, my lord, I am the woman who stood by you here, praying to the LORD. 27 <u>For this child I prayed, and the LORD has granted me my petition which I asked of Him</u>.* – 1 Samuel 1:26-27

2. *O LORD my God, <u>I cried out to You, And You healed me</u>.* – Psalm 30:2

3. *<u>And when they had prayed, the place where they were assembled together was shaken</u>; and they were all filled with the Holy Spirit, and they spoke the word of God with boldness.* – Acts 4:31

4. *Elijah was a man with a nature like ours, and <u>he prayed earnestly that it would not rain</u>; and it did not rain on the land for three years and six months. 18 And he prayed again, and the heaven gave rain, and the earth produced its fruit.* – James 5:17-18

TYPES OF PRAYER

In 1 Timothy 2:1, Paul tells us of four types of prayer: (1) supplications: a petition to God; (2) prayers: an oratory or worshipful prayers to God; (3) intercessions: an interview with God on behalf of others; and (4) giving of thanks: grateful language.

1. **Types of prayers:** *Therefore I exhort first of all that supplications, prayers, intercessions, and giving of thanks be made for all men.* – 1 Timothy 2:1-2

2. **Example of supplications**: *And may You hear the supplications of Your servant and of Your people Israel, when they pray toward this place. Hear from heaven Your dwelling place, and when You hear, forgive.* 2 Chronicles 6:21

3. **Example of worshipful prayers:** *Then another angel, having a golden censer, came and stood at the altar. He was given much incense, that he should offer it with the prayers of all the saints upon the golden altar which was before the throne. And the smoke of the incense, with the prayers of the saints, ascended before God from the angel's hand* – Revelation 8:3-4

4. **Example of intercessions:** *Christ, who died, and furthermore is also risen, who is even at the right hand of God, who makes intercession for us.* – Romans 8:34

5. **Example of giving of thanks:** *For every creature of God is good, and nothing is to be refused if it is received with thanksgiving.* – 1 Timothy 1:4

Questions / Considerations:

- What type of prayers do you think that most people pray? Which type of prayer or prayers do you think would foster more two-way communication between you and God?

PRIVATE AND SOCIAL PRAYER

We should each have personal devotional times of prayer. Private prayer may be verbal or it may be silent, meditative prayer (Genesis 24:63; Psalm 5:1). Jesus instructs that sometimes we should pray in secret (Matthew 6:6). Yet, we should also be actively involved in corporate prayer settings.

1. **Private:** *And when He had sent the multitudes away, He went up on the mountain by Himself to pray.* – Matthew 14:23

2. **Small groups:** *Again, I say to you that if two of you agree on earth concerning anything that they ask, it will be done for them by My Father in heaven. 20 For where two or three are gathered together in My name, I am there in the midst of them.* – Matthew 18:19-20

3. **Corporate settings:** *And when they had entered, they went up into the upper room where they were staying: Peter, James, John, and Andrew; Philip and Thomas; Bartholomew and Matthew; James the son of Alphaeus and Simon the Zealot; and Judas the son of James. 14 These all continued with one accord in prayer and supplication, with the women and Mary the mother of Jesus, and with His brothers.* – Acts 1:13-14

THE WORD OF GOD – THE BIBLE

Another part of a Christian's devotional time should include reading, studying, and mediating on the Word of God – the Bible. Here are examples of why it is so important.

1. **It teaches us about Jesus Christ:** (NIV) *The gospel he promised beforehand through his prophets in the Holy Scriptures 3 regarding his Son, who as to his human nature was a descendant of David, 4 and who through the Spirit of holiness was declared with power to be the Son of God by his resurrection from the dead: Jesus Christ our Lord.* – Romans 1:2-4

2. **It gives us the words of Jesus Christ:** *Let the word of Christ dwell in you richly in all wisdom, teaching and admonishing one another in psalms and hymns and spiritual songs, singing with grace in your hearts to the Lord.* – Colossians 3:16-17

3. **It is God-breathed and useful for every good work:** (NIV) All *Scripture is God-breathed and is useful for teaching,*

74

rebuking, correcting and training in righteousness, 17 so that the man of God may be thoroughly equipped for every good work. − 2 Timothy 3:16-17

4. **It pierces the soul and spirit:** *For the word of God is living and powerful, and sharper than any two-edged sword, <u>piercing even to the division of soul and spirit</u>, and of joints and marrow, and is a discerner of the thoughts and intents of the heart.* − Hebrews 4:12-13

5. **It is the book of truth:** (NIV) *So he said, "Do you know why I have come to you? Soon I will return to fight against the prince of Persia, and when I go, the prince of Greece will come; 21 but first I will tell you what is written in the Book of Truth.* − Dan 10:20-21

6. **It is the sword of the Spirit:** *And take the helmet of salvation, and the sword of the Spirit, which is the word of God.* − Ephesians 6:17-18

7. **It brings a blessing:** *Blessed is he who reads and those who hear the words of this prophecy, and keep those things which are written in it; for the time is near.* − Revelation 1:3

8. **It brings us close to God:** *In the beginning was the Word, and the Word was with God, and the Word was God.* − John 1:1-2

Questions / Considerations:

- Do you have a favorite passage of Scripture? Share it with the group. Do you have a favorite book in the Bible? What is it? What has the Bible done for you in your life?

8: Everyday Christian Living: Part Two

And He said to him, "Arise, go your way.
Your faith has made you well." - Luke 17:19

Activity: Take a moment to quickly review the lesson titles in the table of contents, or briefly flip through the pages of the lessons to review. What are one or two things that you have learned from these lessons so far that have helped you in your understanding or in your walk with the Lord?

Note: In this final lesson, we will conclude by briefly taking into account some other areas that are important in our daily living as Christians.

DISCIPLESHIP

We are called to be disciples. The word *disciple* is found hundreds of times in the New Testament; the word *Christian* only a few. The basic meaning of disciple is "learner" or "pupil". The word *disciple* is associated with the word *discipline.* The call to Christians is for them to become disciplined followers of the Lord Jesus Christ. Whereas a student learns what his teacher knows, a disciple becomes what his master is and then passes it on to others.

1. **The call:** *Then He said to them, "Follow Me, and I will make you fishers of men." –* Matthew 4:19

2. **Become like Jesus:** *A disciple is not above his teacher, but everyone who is perfectly trained will be like his teacher. –* Luke 6:40

3. **Spreading the word:** *Then the word of God spread, and the number of the disciples multiplied greatly in Jerusalem, and a great many of the priests were obedient to the faith. –* Acts 6:7

76

4. **The name Christian:** *And when he had found him, he brought him to Antioch. So, it was that for a whole year they assembled with the church and taught a great many people. And the disciples were first called Christians in Antioch.* – Acts 11:26

5. **Missions:** *Go therefore and make disciples of all the nations, baptizing them in the name of the Father and of the Son and of the Holy Spirit, 20 teaching them to observe all things that I have commanded you; and lo, I am with you always, even to the end of the age."* Amen. – Matthew 28:19-20

SERVING

We are called to be servants. Jesus was our example as a servant. He told us to serve Him and others.

1. **Right attitude:** *But Jesus called them to Himself and said to them, "You know that those who are considered rulers over the Gentiles lord it over them, and their great ones exercise authority over them. 43 Yet it shall not be so among you; but whoever desires to become great among you shall be your servant. 44 And whoever of you desires to be first shall be slave of all. 45 For even the Son of Man did not come to be served, but to serve, and to give His life a ransom for many.* – Mark 10:42-45

2. **Honor from God:** *If anyone serves Me, let him follow Me; and where I am, there My servant will be also. If anyone serves Me, him My Father will honor.* – John 12:26

3. **Example of Phoebe:** *I commend to you Phoebe our sister, who is a servant of the church in Cenchrea, 2 that you may receive her in the Lord in a manner worthy of the saints, and assist her in whatever business she has need of you; for indeed she has been a helper of many and of myself also.* – Romans 16:1-2

4. **Example of Paul:** *For though I am free from all men, I have made myself a servant to all, that I might win the more.* – 1 Corinthians 9:19

5. **Servant's example:** *And a servant of the Lord must not quarrel but be gentle to all, able to teach, patient, 25 in humility correcting those who are in opposition, if God perhaps will grant them repentance, so that they may know the truth, 26 and that they may come to their senses and escape the snare of the devil, having been taken captive by him to do his will.* – 2 Timothy 2:24-26

Questions / Considerations:

- In what areas of discipleship and serving would you like to grow? Can you think of some specific areas in which you would like to grow in the next several months?

WORSHIPING

We are called to be worshippers. Worship is not confined to church services and is not just about singing and music, though that can be an expression of it. Worship is giving reverence to God with our lives.

1. **Give glory:** <u>*Give unto the LORD the glory*</u> *due to His name; worship the LORD in the beauty of holiness.* – Psalm 29:2

2. **Singing:** *All the earth shall worship You and* <u>*sing praises to You*</u>*; they shall sing praises to Your name.* – Psalm 66:4

3. **Bowing:** *Oh come, let us worship and bow down;* <u>*let us kneel*</u> *before the LORD our Maker.* – Psalm 95:6

4. **Musical instruments:** *Praise Him with stringed* <u>*instruments*</u> *and flutes!* – Psalm 150:4

5. **In spirit and truth:** *But the hour is coming, and now is, when the true worshipers will worship the Father in spirit and truth; for the Father is seeking such to worship Him. 24* <u>*God is Spirit, and those who worship Him must worship in spirit and truth*</u>. - John 4:23-24

CHURCH GATHERINGS

The word *church* means "called out ones" and is used dozens of times in the New Testament. It is those called by Christ to follow Him, and it normally refers to the assembling of those who are called. Jesus used the term to refer to the universal church (Matthew 16:18) as well as a local church (Matthew 18:17). Many things happen in the gathering of the saints: corporate worship, teaching, praying, salvation, communion, etc. Here are just a few aspects of church life.

1. **Growth:** *And the Lord added to the church daily those who were being saved.* – Acts 2:47

2. **Leadership:** *So when they had appointed elders in every church, and prayed with fasting, they commended them to the Lord in whom they had believed.* – Acts 14:23

3. **Edification:** *He who prophesies edifies the church.* – 1 Corinthians 14:4

4. **Stirring up love and good works:** *And let us consider one another in order to stir up love and good works, 25 not forsaking the assembling of ourselves together, as is the manner of some, but exhorting one another, and so much the more as you see the Day approaching.* – Hebrews 10:24-25

5. **Prayer:** *Is anyone among you sick? Let him call for the elders of the church, and let them pray over him, anointing him with oil in the name of the Lord.* – James 5:14

Questions / Considerations:

- What is one of your favorite things about gathering with other Christians?

FAMILY

In the lesson on love, we discussed this important area. Love is first and foremost, but here are some other significant aspects.

1. **Children:** (AMP) *Children, obey your parents in the Lord [as His representatives], for this is just and right.* – Ephesians 6:1

2. **Fathers:** (AMP) *Fathers, do not irritate and provoke your children to anger – do not exasperate them to resentment – but rear them [tenderly] in the training and discipline and the counsel and admonition of the Lord.* – Ephesians 6:4

79

3. **Wives:** (AMP) *Wives, be subject – be submissive and adapt yourselves – to your own husbands as [a service] to the Lord.* – Ephesians 5:22

4. **Husbands:** (AMP) *In the same way you married men should live considerably with [your wives], with an intelligent recognition [of the marriage relation], honoring the woman as [physically] the weaker, but [realizing that you] are joint heirs of the grace (God's unmerited favor) of life, in order that your prayers may not be hindered and cut off. – Otherwise, you cannot pray effectively.* – 1 Peter 3:7

WORK

There are many aspects of work and career, yet here are a few things that the Bible tells us consider.

1. **Treating employees with kindness:** *Now behold, Boaz came from Bethlehem, and said to the reapers, "The LORD be with you!" And they answered him, "The LORD bless you!"* – Ruth 2:4

2. **Workers deserve to get paid:** *For the Scripture says, "You shall not muzzle an ox while it treads out the grain," and, "The laborer is worthy of his wages."* – 1 Timothy 5:18

3. **Wages should be fair:** *Masters, give your bondservants what is just and fair, knowing that you also have a Master in heaven.* – Colossians 4:1

4. **Working diligently:** (AMP) *Whatever may be your task, work at it heartily (from the soul), as [something done] for the Lord and not men.* – Colossians 3:23

5. **Doing what is right:** *Let him who stole steal no longer, but rather let him labor, working with his hands what is good, that he may have something to give him who has need.* – Ephesians 4:28-29

6. **The need for rest:** *Six days you shall labor and do all your work, 14 but the seventh day is the Sabbath of the LORD your God. In it you shall do no work.* – Deuteronomy 5:13-14

COMMUNICATION

We are to be careful with our communication.

1. (NIV) *Without wood a fire goes out; without gossip a quarrel dies down.* – Proverbs 26:20

2. *Let no corrupt word proceed out of your mouth, but what is good for necessary edification, that it may impart grace to the hearers.* – Ephesians 4:29

3. (TLB) *Dirty stories, foul talk, and coarse jokes-these are not for you. Instead, remind each other of God's goodness, and be thankful.* – Ephesians 5:4

4. *Let your speech always be with grace, seasoned with salt, that you may know how you ought to answer each one.* – Colossians 4:6

5. *Out of the same mouth proceed blessing and cursing. My brethren, these things ought not to be so.* – James 3:10

Questions / Considerations:

- Have you ever started to say something and then realized that it is improper? When we start to say things that we regret, what are some ways to stop or graciously move away from the improper comment?

FINANCES

Christians should be good stewards of what God has given to us. We should put faith in God's desire and ability to provide for our needs, seek Him for whatever we need, and be generous with tithes, offerings for projects, missions, etc., and alms for the poor.

1. **Honoring God:** *Honor the LORD with your possessions, and with the first fruits of all your increase; 10 So your barns will be filled with plenty, and your vats will overflow with new wine.* – Proverbs 3:9-10

2. **Tithe and blessings:** *Bring all the tithes into the storehouse, that there may be food in My house, and try Me now in this," says the LORD of hosts, "If I will not open for you the windows*

of heaven and pour out for you such blessing that there will not be room enough to receive it. – Malachi 3:10

3. **Seeking God:** *Ask, and it will be given to you; seek, and you will find; knock, and it will be opened to you. 8 For everyone who asks receives, and he who seeks finds, and to him who knocks it will be opened. 9 Or what man is there among you who, if his son asks for bread, will give him a stone? 10 Or if he asks for a fish, will he give him a serpent? 11 If you then, being evil, know how to give good gifts to your children, how much more will your Father who is in heaven give good things to those who ask Him! – Matthew 7:7-12*

4. **God supplying all needs:** *And my God shall supply all your need according to His riches in glory by Christ Jesus. – Philippians 4:19*

5. **Faithfulness:** *Moreover it is required in stewards that one be found faithful. – 1 Corinthians 4:2*

6. **Sharing:** *As each one has received a gift, minister it to one another, as good stewards of the manifold grace of God. – 1 Peter 4:10*

7. **Contentment:** *Now godliness with contentment is great gain. 7 For we brought nothing into this world, and it is certain we can carry nothing out. 8 And having food and clothing, with these we shall be content. 9 But those who desire to be rich fall into temptation and a snare, and into many foolish and harmful lusts which drown men in destruction and perdition. 10 For the love of money is a root of all kinds of evil, for which some have strayed from the faith in their greediness, and pierced themselves through with many sorrows. – 1 Timothy 6:6-10*

8. **Cheerful giver:** *But this I say: He who sows sparingly will also reap sparingly, and he who sows bountifully will also reap bountifully. 7 So let each one give as he purposes in his heart, not grudgingly or of necessity; for God loves a cheerful giver. 8 And God is able to make all grace abound toward you, that you, always having all sufficiency in all things, may have an abundance for every good work. – 2 Corinthians 9"6-9*

Questions / Considerations:

- Why do you think that God made money such an important part of our lives? It appears that when we are generous with what we have, God blesses us even more so. Why is that?

CHARACTER

There are numerous righteous characteristics that we should embrace. Here are several that we may find need for on a daily or weekly basis.

1. **Honesty:** *Behold, You desire truth in the inward parts, and in the hidden part You will make me to know wisdom.* – Psalm 51:6

2. **Purity:** *How can a young man cleanse his way? By taking heed according to Your word.* – Psalm 119:9

3. **Faithfulness:** *He who is faithful in what is least is faithful also in much.* – Luke 16:10

4. **Honor:** *Honor all people. Love the brotherhood. Fear God. Honor the king.* – 1 Peter 2:17

5. **Endurance:** *Let us run with endurance the race that is set before us.* – Hebrews 12:1

6. **Humility:** *Humble yourselves in the sight of the Lord, and He will lift you up.* – James 4:10

Questions / Considerations:

- Which one of these characteristics speaks to you the most? Are there others not listed here that are really important to you?

SHINING YOUR LIGHT

Christians are called to shine the light of Jesus Christ into our homes, work places, ministries, and community.

1. *You are the light of the world. A city that is set on a hill cannot be hidden. 15 Nor do they light a lamp and put it under a basket, but on a lamp stand, and it gives light to all who are in the house. 16 Let your light so shine before men, that they may see your good works and glorify your Father in heaven.* – Matthew 5:14-16

2. *But you be watchful in all things, endure afflictions, do the work of an evangelist, fulfill your ministry.* – 2 Timothy 4:5

3. *The fruit of the righteous is a tree of life, and he who wins souls is wise.* – Proverbs 11:30

4. *Do all things without complaining and disputing, 15 that you may become blameless and harmless, children of God without fault in the midst of a crooked and perverse generation, among whom you shine as lights in the world.* - Philippians 2:14-15

5. *For you were once darkness, but now you are light in the Lord. Walk as children of light.* – Ephesians 5:8

6. *But the path of the just is like the shining sun, that shines ever brighter unto the perfect day.* – Proverbs 4:18

Questions / Considerations:

- The Lord will lead you into a path of brilliance. He will help you learn how to shine your light in the best way possible.

- Pray that the Lord will give strength to each one in the group to live in such a way that it glorifies God and shines His light before others.

www.ingramcontent.com/pod-product-compliance
Lightning Source LLC
Chambersburg PA
CBHW060532030426
42337CB00021B/4216